D0764065

RETURN TO
SBVMWD
ENG. LIBRARY

RETURN TO
DRAWING
ENG. LIBRARY

SIMPLIFIED ACCOUNTING FOR ENGINEERING AND TECHNICAL CONSULTANTS

Small Business Management Series
Rick Stephan Hayes, Editor

Simplified Accounting for Non-Accountants
 by Rick Stephan Hayes and C. Richard Baker

How to Finance Your Small Business with Government Money: SBA Loans
 by Rick Stephan Hayes and John Cotton Howell

Accounting for Small Manufacturers
 by C. Richard Baker and Rick Stephan Hayes

Simplified Accounting for Engineering and Technical Consultants
 by Rick Stephan Hayes and C. Richard Baker

SIMPLIFIED ACCOUNTING FOR ENGINEERING AND TECHNICAL CONSULTANTS

RICK STEPHAN HAYES

C. RICHARD BAKER

OCLC# 6087795   3/13/95

A Ronald Press Publication

JOHN WILEY & SONS

New York   •   Chichester   •   Brisbane   •   Toronto

Copyright © 1980 by John Wiley & Sons, Inc.

All rights reserved. Published simultaneously in Canada.

Reproduction or translation of any part of this work
beyond that permitted by Sections 107 or 108 of the
1976 United States Copyright Act without the permission
of the copyright owner is unlawful. Requests for
permission or further information should be addressed to
the Permissions Department, John Wiley & Sons, Inc.

This publication is designed to provide accurate and
authoritative information in regard to the subject
matter covered. It is sold with the understanding that
the publisher is not engaged in rendering legal, accounting,
or other professional service. If legal advice or other
expert assistance is required, the services of a competent
professional person should be sought. *From a Declaration
of Principles jointly adopted by a Committee of the
American Bar Association and a Committee of Publishers.*

Library of Congress Cataloging in Publication Data

Hayes, Rick Stephan, 1946-
    Simplified accounting for engineering and technical
consultants.

    (Wiley series on small business management)
    "A Ronald Press publication."
    Includes index.
    1. Accounting.   I. Baker, C. Richard, 1946-
joint author.   II. Title.   III. Series.

HF5635.H413   657   80-12360
ISBN 0-471-05708-8

Printed in the United States of America

10 9 8 7 6 5 4 3 2 1

To my engineer-type friends

Ed Cernek, Gar Wilson, Bob Denny, Glen Gray, and Rod Waters

Preface

An engineer looks for the practical. A technical consultant looks to the necessary. This is the nature of these professions. This book, therefore, approaches accounting from a practical standpoint. Yet nothing essential to the understanding of accounting is left undescribed.

Other accounting books have approached accounting with an academic bias. Academically, the exceptions are as important as the rules, and the special cases get the most attention. But we believe that an accounting rule that applies only to 1/100 of America's businesses should be left out. Here we concentrate on the basics. Here we emphasize the practical and logical solutions.

In the real business world you are literally adrift without a basic knowledge of accounting. What is worse, your lack of knowledge may cost you hard cash, theft, imprecise inventory, inaccurate accounts receivable, or uncontrollable expenses.

But to learn how things work in the real world, it is best to see through the eyes of someone in a situation similar to your own. This book is written from the viewpoint of Lazarus Time, an engineer in the electronics industry who has just started two businesses. One business is a consulting company with himself as the primary asset and employee. The other business he owns is a manufacturing business in the special laser market. This manufacturing business is run by him and his partner who together invented a holographic memory storage device. He knows that he can postpone learning about accounting no longer.

How Lazarus Time learns about accounting through lectures, reading, discussion, and, finally, keeping his own journals and ledgers is the story told in this book. This book shows how Lazarus Time learns about accounting and then applies what he learns to his businesses.

This book consists of an accounting survival kit made up of material about:

- Recording hourly time expenditures
- Proper billing techniques
- Investment tax credits
- Recordkeeping
- Journals
- Ledgers
- Double-entry accounting
- Income statements
- Balance sheets
- Financial forecasts
- Assets
- Liabilities and debt
- Equity under different business organizations

- Income and fees
- Cost of sales
- Inventory management
- Tax deductible expenses
- Tax treatment of corporations
- Accounts receivable records
- Increasing collections
- Loans
- Budgeting
- Cash management techniques
- Depreciation
- Bad debt
- Travel expenses
- Forms of business organizations
- Sub-chapter S corporations
- Partnership accounting
- Special financial ratios
- Wages
- Trial balances
- Accounting workpapers
- Managerial finance techniques

The purpose, intent, and goal of this book is to make accounting easier to understand in the real world. We hope you enjoy it.

Topanga Canyon, California   Rick Stephan Hayes
New York, New York   C. Richard Baker
March 1980

Contents

Chapter One

Accounting for Engineering and Technical Consultants

"To you, what does self-sctualization mean?" the instructor asked.

Laz smiled. "To be *president* of my own company," he answered. "To be the boss. That's freedom. That's the answer."

Lazarus Time has always wanted to be president. Ever since he could remember. He had always wanted two things: to be president and to work with electronic gadgets. When he was six years old he knew that RADAR was an acronym. When he was twelve years old and the other kids were talking about becoming lawyers, firemen, and carpenters, he wanted to be president of General Motors.

All through his childhood he studied radar, hoping to be a radar engineer when he finished college. By the time he started college, he realized that the future in radar was not as unlimited as he had dreamed it would be. But he saw another acronym that was attractive—LASER.

In college he did a thesis on lasers and their future. He was hooked. When he graduated, he went to work for a large aerospace firm, like so many other engineers of that period—the 1960s.

He worked on the space program and made a brilliant discovery or two while developing a computer flight tracking program. He soon became bored with the space program. When they moved his department into the old company buildings, he knew his number was up. At his company they only moved you to the old buildings—the oncs overlooking the chemical dump—when they couldn't find any work for you.

He started polishing up his resumé and applied to companies that were in the laser industry. Since almost all the companies in the industry at that time—the late 1960s—were small, his resume and experience helped land him a job with one of the big innovators in the field. He got a job as a design engineer with the same company he had researched for his thesis in college, Lascomco.

Laz could never be called dumb. He knew that the engineering profession was pretty much a dead end in itself. He worked a deal with Lascomco to do some after hours work in the marketing department. The company was small enough, and he was determined enough, and it didn't cost anyone anything.

Lazarus Time met the salesmen and got to know them well. He learned the sales procedures. He discovered how to market effectively through the use of brochures. He went to the trade shows.

Most important of all he learned that the questions asked about a product by the purchaser were different from those asked by engineers.

Before Laz would even begin to design a brochure, he would call as many of the potential purchasers as he could and ask them what questions they had about the product. He took the questions that they asked and designed the brochures to answer only these questions. He also found that the people who signed the checks didn't ask the same questions as the engineers.

All this marketing know-how seeped into his knowledge over a period of years. Two years after he started putzing around the marketing department, Lazcomco made Lazarus its director of marketing.

But it was only four years later, six full years after he started to work for Lascomco, that Laz stumbled into something that would eventually allow him to go into business for himself as a consultant. Laz noticed that one of Lascomco's biggest customers was ordering a large number of laser tubes to be sent to Ohio.

The purchasing manager wouldn't tell Laz what they were using the laser tubes for. This reticence was very unusual in the industry. Laz knew that something was cooking.

After six months of clever detective work—checking invoices, cross checking with other suppliers, and reading the papers of the researchers at the customer firm—Laz knew.

They were using the large number of tubes as part of a research grant to make commercial holographic memories for data collection.

Laz was overjoyed. At last he had found a gadget that was just in the first stages of development. He realized the potential for holographic memories. Holography held promise as a means of storing data and information. It could become a basis of memory whose large capacity and permanence might overcome the deficiencies of the more conventional storage techniques.

The next day Laz took off work and went to the library. He had to do some research. Holography was discovered in 1948 by Dr. Dennis Gabor while he worked to improve the resolution of the electron microscope. It is a method for recording an object on film by capturing the interference pattern of light waves bouncing off it. But holography did not find any practical application until the laser was developed in the 1960s. The laser provides a source of "coherent" light—light with waves that were all the same wave length and in phase. This is the ingredient needed in holography to produce good interference patterns. Holography is a high density information recording technique using optical image coding.

The holography technology offered a high data storage capacity that would make microfilm obsolete. If holography could be combined with the new Computer Output Microfiche (COM) systems, the possibilities would look very good.

Whenever there was a holography conference in his state, Laz would take off work and go to it. Pretty soon he realized that the same old people went to all of these conferences. Holography was indeed a small world.

Laz and a fellow that he met at one of the conferences, Ignatz Culver Whiz, went in together to buy the necessary components to experiment with holography. After a few years of work (which was really just like playing with a toy) the boys got together a pretty good system.

At the same time that Lazarus Time and I. C. Whiz were trying to decide on the marketability of their system, a strange coincidence occurred.

Ignatz was anxious to put the holography system that they had devised on the market. But right now the system consisted of a whole series of integrated circuits and components hooked together and there was no fancy prototype to show the customers. Ignatz knew that if they had another $30,000 to $40,000, they could get the prototype out and start a company.

One day when Ignatz was sitting at the kitchen table trying to figure out the cost of integrating some of his components, he received a phone call.

The person calling was a great aunt who informed Ignatz that his great uncle had died, leaving him an inheritance. The matter was being handled by the family attorney and would take six months to a year to resolve, but the amount of the bequest might be from $100,000 to $250,000 in cash. His aunt said that he should be getting a letter to this effect soon.

Only two hours before I. C. Whiz received this fateful call from his great aunt, Lazarus Time was talking to the senior vice president of a very large electronics firm that was in the Fortune 500. Laz was offered a job to come to the company as sales director for their new holographic division.

Laz didn't accept on the spot, of course, but he was overjoyed. It was the most positive step he could take in his life ambition to be president of a company.

When I. C. Whiz and Lazarus Time told each other about these events, they knew there was going to be a problem. They had the chance to start their own company, but Laz now had an offer for a big job.

The problem was finally resolved: they would still start their own company but Ignatz would be the president and take a salary. Laz, on the other hand, would work when he could and bill his hours to the company at a reasonable rate. They would own the company 50-50, but Ignatz would make all administrative decisions. This arrangement allowed them to start the company and Laz to accept the job by the Fortune 500 firm. Laz would put up $10,000 of his money and Ignatz would put up $10,000. Whatever other money the company needed would be loaned by Ignatz to the company at the prevailing interest rate.

Laz wanted to be totally fair and accurate about reporting his hours to his partner, Ignatz, because it was important to him. They decided to call their new company W.T. Technologies.

One day Ignatz met an old high school buddy who was in the consulting business. Ignatz told his consultant friend that Laz was going to bill his hours to W.T. Technologies and wanted to know the means and techniques. The consultant gave Ignatz a copy of an article that had appeared in a trade magazine. Ignatz read it and gave it to Laz. Here is how it read. . . .

TIME ACCOUNTING AND FEES

I think I can safely say that the most important accounting item to a business consultant is the fees he or she receives. Fees are paid to the consultant for the time he or she has expended. Therefore it becomes very important that these billed hours are carefully accounted for and carefully presented, and that their payment is actively pursued.

What Time and Expenses Should be Recorded?

Before time expended to assist a client can be billed, it first must be accounted for. Expenses incurred on behalf of the client should be carefully noted.

First, it is important to consider the question: "What time should I keep track of?" Should you keep track of just the time you expend in direct, hands-on work for the client? Should you also include telephone conversation time? Travel time? Research time? Time spent socializing with the client?

My opinion is that no matter what time you decide to finally bill, you should keep track of *all* time that you spent with or for the client. You should record each and every telephone conversation: date, time, and summary of what was discussed. You should record all time spent traveling between your business or home and the client-designated meeting place. You should even record every hour you spent with the client "socializing" at cocktail parties, dinners, nights on the town, or whatever.

"Why make records of all these times if, in fact, I don't plan to bill for these hours?" you may ask. There are three good reasons for this extensive accounting for hours:

1. Accounting for *all* time spent on a client (before, during, and after work hours and on the telephone) gives you the most accurate picture of real amount of time spent with a client.
2. It gives the client a complete accounting of what they spent their money for. Accounting for all the time lets you list the complete time you spent for the client on your bill (even though some hours expended were not charged to the client).
3. In the event of an eventual court action to recover fees, you have the advantage of being able to present to the court all the facts of the case in more than adequate detail.

Business consultants often perform time-consuming services for their clients at "no charge" but fail to notify the client. The irony of this is that the uninformed client not only fails to appreciate these "extras" but often will later accuse the consultant of overcharging. No charge services may include giving valuable advice over the phone not directly related to the project, special memoranda, reports, background searches of clients, and other "behind the scenes" services. Such services include discussing the case with other professionals to get their opinions and "feeling out" bankers, IRS agents, or government officials. If these extras are not noted, their value will never be seen.

Similarly all expenses incurred on behalf of the client should be recorded, and original transaction documents such as receipts should be retained. This would especially be true if you are charging expenses to the client.

All expenses should be recorded including:

- Telephone calls on client's behalf.
- Parking when in the field.
- Luncheons with the client or their personnel.
- Automobile use and expense.
- Travel expenses.
- Postage, duplicating, binding, and supplies.
- Typing, accounting, legal, technical, or other "outside services."

Recording Time and Expense

The four records used by business consultants to keep track of time and expenses expended for the benefit of the client are:

1. The consultant's appointment book.
2. A written summary of the hours employed by client which I call "Summary of Hours Expended."
3. A summary of all telephone conversations.
4. A summary of expenses incurred on behalf of that client.

The last three documents—hours summary, telephone conversation summary, and expense summary—may be incorporated into one document or each may be separate.

Almost every businessperson maintains an *appointment calendar*. These are available in every shape and size and for all tastes. In this appointment calendar, you will keep track of the times and days of appointments with all your clients. Figure 1.1 is a sample appointment book page.

A summary of hours expended can be kept in a spiral notebook or other simple bound book. The essential elements in the summary are the date, the time expended, and a short summary of the activity performed. The summary of hours extended is usually kept by the individual consultant and updated in longhand. See Figure 1.2 for a sample page from a summary of hours extended book.

Telephone conversation summaries may be in the form of a spiral or steno notebook. The important elements are the date, the name of the person with whom the conversation was held, who called whom, a summary of what was said, and the length of the conversation. Figure 1.3 is an sample page from a telephone conversation summary.

A *summary of expenses* need only be a list of the items expensed, the date, and the amount. Figure 1.4 shows a sample expense schedule.

```
DATE:  _____        LUNCH APPOINTMENT
       _____
  TO SEE                     PERSONAL
  ----------------------     ----------------------
  -                          -
  -                          -
  -                          -
  -                          -
  -                          -
  ----------------------     ----------------------
  PROJECTS                   TO WRITE
  ----------------------     ----------------------
  -                          -
  -                          -
  -                          -
  -                          -
  -                          -
  -                          -
  TO PHONE                   -
  ----------------------     ----------------------
  -                          EXPENSES
  -                          ----------------------
  -
  -
  -                          ----------------------
  -                          APPOINTMENTS
  -                          ----------------------
  -                          -
  -                          -
  -                          -
  -                          -
  -
```

Figure 1.1.   Copy of a page of an appointment book.

YOURCOMPANY
SUMMARY OF HOURS p 3

Date	Hrs	Comments
1/17/79	5.47	At Yourcompany factory prepared schedule of their largest customers; inspected business operations; and reviewed market material on future K-25 Zammer purchases. Travel 1 hr - 1 minute.
1/18/79	1.25	Telephone conversations w/ John Your (27 min); Edward Jars of CCSP (25 minutes); and Pete Popstein, CPA (23min) See Telephone Call Summary, pp 72 & 73
1/21/79	0.75	Review Yourcompany notes, call Edward Jars and John Your to remind them of meetings (see Call Summary p 77)
1/23/79	1.50	At CCSP met with Edward Jars. Discussed new K-25 Zammer, then

Figure 1.2.   Sample of a summary of hours extended book.

Billing the Client

Billing the client is a crucial activity that should receive more care and concern than it usually does. Remember, the bill is the chief document that shows the client if he or she got his or her money's worth or not.

There are two concerns in billing: (1) what hours and expenses are billed to the client, and (2) what should the bill look like?

Each individual business consultant and firm may have a different idea of what hours should be billed to the client. Some feel that the client should be billed only for the time spent "hands on" with the project. Some feel that travel and telephoning time should be included. Some include expenses. Other companies don't. Still others have the operating philosophy that the client should be billed for all expenses and hours recorded. This is a decision that each consulting firm should make. The client should be told of the firm's policy from the start so there will be no misunderstanding. The important thing is that whatever policy your company chooses, you must be consistent. It is problematic to charge one client with telephone hours and not charge another client.

Figure 1.5 is a puzzle. Is the center rectangle in the two illustrations the same size or is one center rectangle larger than the other?

Most people would say that the rectangle in the bottom illustration is larger. In fact both center rectangles are the same size. The bottom rectangle *looks* larger because it is surrounded by smaller rectangles. The top center rectangle looks smaller because it is surrounded by bigger rectangles.

The point that I am making is that the way a customer sees your fees depends on what surrounds the final dollar amount. If you present a client with a bill on your

Call Summary p 72

1/18/79 John Your called. Discussed yesterday's visit. I told him he had a 57 day receivable period. Discussed marketing data I had reviewed and reviewed. Made appointment to meet 1/23 @ 9:30 @ Your-company. Time: 10:51-11:18 - 27 min.

1/18/79 Called Edward Jaro of CCSP. Asked him about design of Yourcompany #2 production line. He said: "Controlled by H.P. 8 bit test machine; Thompson belts; three work stations; said major problem was bottle-neck at second work station. Set up appointment for 1/22 @ 3:00 @ CCSP Time: 11:30-11:55 - 25 minutes

1/18/79 Called Pete Popstein, CPA for Yourcompany. He said that the financial statements should be

Figure 1.3. Copy of a telephone conversation summary.

EXPENSE SUMMARY

Date	Amount	Item
1/15/81	$ 2.50	Parking @ Yourcompany
1/15/81	8.50	Office supplies
1/16/81	1.20	12 copies @ 10¢ ea.
1/17/81	2.50	Parking @ Yourcompany
1/17/81	7.63	Lunch
1/22/79	1.75	Parking @ CCSP
1/23/79	2.50	Parking @ Yourcompany
1/23/79	7.18	Lunch

Sub-total $33.76

1/25/79 2.00 Parking @ Popstein's

Figure 1.4. Copy of an expense schedule.

letterhead that says "Fees for services rendered—$1500" with no other explanation, he or she will get an entirely different concept of value than if he or she receives an itemized list. If the same bill has two pages of dates, hours, explanations, itemization of expenses, and so on, the client will consider that he or she got something for his or her money.

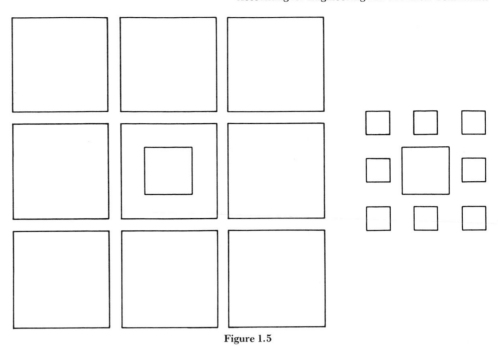

Figure 1.5

Without a doubt, a large dollar figure for professional services standing by itself, without explanation or amplification, is a wide open invitation to criticism. Many overcharging complaints may be traced to this all-in-one method of billing.

To many people $700 in lawyer's fees for incorporating a company, representing such simple procedures as "having his secretary fill out the forms" seems exorbitant.

A detailed, itemized bill for legal services for incorporation could look like this:

- 3/16/83 and 3/23/83: Conferences with client and accountant re: corporation structure.
- 3/25/83: Prepared articles of incorporation, secured their execution, and filed to secure charter.
- 5/30/83: Prepared bylaws and corporation record book, including minutes of incorporation meeting, first meeting of stockholders and board of directors.
- 6/12/83: Prepared and issued stock certificates.

Total hours
Total billing $1000.00

We have all received bills for professional services. We all know how it feels to receive a lump sum bill without any detail explanation. A lump sum bill implies that you don't care, that the client can take it or leave it, or that you have padded the bill and don't want to let the client know.

An itemized bill tells the client that you care and want to give him or her a complete accounting of your time and that you are charging a reasonable amount for services rendered.

Basis of Fees

Fees may be based on a flat fee, an hourly rate, or a monthly retainer. The best arrangement is a matter of taste, competition, and sometimes government regulation.

The flat fee offers the advantage of allowing the client to know the cost in advance. If the service for which you charge a flat fee requires an unpredictable amount of time, the flat fee may bring in less money than an hourly rate. In some areas of business consulting the flat fee is standard, therefore the business consultant doesn't have much choice.

The important thing to consider when setting a flat fee is how much time the task is likely to take you. When estimating the time it will take, it is prudent to be conservative. A business acquaintance always tells me, "I make my most conservative estimate of what time it will take me, then double it."

The hourly rate fee is the fairest to both consultant and client. The client isn't charged for time not needed and the consultant gets a fair return for every hour he spends. Hourly rate charges are easier to keep track of and provide a good data base if you ever want to do cost-benefit analysis.

The monthly retainer is used only in rare cases where the client continually uses a consultant's time. The advantages and disadvantages of a monthly retainer vary from case to case. But remember, you should be reimbursed at a rate roughly equivalent to what you would have received had you charged hourly rates.

Many consultants have different hourly rates for different tasks, and for different people. A tax-expert general partner in a consulting firm might receive $300 per hour whereas auditing time of a new employee might be charged at $25 per hour. The Small Business Administration in Los Angeles has a whole task-rate structure for people who assist SBA loan applicants in preparing a loan application—$35 per hour of consultation, $25 per hour for financial analysis, and $12.50 for clerical work.

Collection of Fees

The method you use to bill your fees can directly affect collection of those fees. If you bill completely in advance (which is hard to do), you have no collection problems. On the other hand, if you bill 100% on completion and don't follow up, you may never collect.

When possible it is a good idea to get at least partial payment in advance. This gives you working capital for expenses and assures that you'll at least be partially compensated.

If the business consultant provides a document at the end of the consulting period—financial statement, market analysis, management recommendation, documentation of a computer system—it is a good idea to receive the balance of payment on presentation of this document. If the client needs the document he will be more willing to pay *before* he receives the document than *after*.

In a fee situation the client always tries to delay payment and the consultant always wants payment as soon as possible. This many times calls for compromise. Partial payments over a several month period may serve that purpose.

Billing the client monthly is a traditional billing technique. If the work is ongoing this will generally assure that the client will not delay payment for more than a month. However, the last monthly billing, after the service has been completed, may require a long time to collect.

Of all businesses, the service industries have the most difficulty collecting their sales. In retailing, wholesaling, and manufacturing, there is a physical product that may be taken back if payment is not made. With service, the hours and services charged for are generally consumed even before the bill is received. If the client wanted a market analysis and he or she now has it, why does he or she need the business consultant who prepared it? Payment for services is generally at the bottom of the list of priorities of the client. A business consultant must be very careful about collecting.

Someone in as precarious a position as the business consultant cannot depend on luck or the good humour of the client to pay the fees that pay the bills. One of the most difficult and necessary steps of any business consultant is collecting. He or she cannot afford the luxury of waiting one month before sending out notices. The business consultant must stay in daily or weekly contact with the client until the fees are paid. In short, sometimes he or she must risk annoying the client to get the money.

Collection Alternatives

If you as a business consultant have trouble collecting your fees from a client after two or three months, you could consider some of the legal alternatives available to you.

If the fee that you cannot collect is $1000 or under, you might consider small claims court. This alternative requires no legal fees and only a small filing fee.

If the fee is over $1000 and your best efforts have not yielded a response, you have no alternative but to hire counsel and pursue the collection in court.

The most important legal advantage you will have if you must pursue collection in court is a contract between your company and the client. A contract will spell out the fee schedule and the schedule of payment, and will establish both your client's and your rights in rendering the proposed service.

I cannot recommend the use of contracts enough! In business consulting it is not a question of whether an occasion will arise when you are not paid your fees, it is a question of when. Have a competent attorney draw up a standard contract for your company now if you do not already have one!

Chapter Two
Accounting and Balance

Lazarus Time and Ignatz Culver Whiz continued with their experimentation in holographs. In no time W.T. Technilogies had been founded and they had an order for their holographic memory system from a large company. The purchaser had agree to pay $40,000 for each unit including tape. Their cost to build the prototype was only $30,000, so they could actually make a bit of money on their first unit.

Lazarus took the job with the Fortune 500 firm—Megatric, Inc.—as director of holographic marketing. There were problems, of course. Laz met the president of Megatric, Inc. on the first day he went to work. It was now six months later and Laz hadn't seen the man again. Megatric had eight different holographic departments going, and only one was producing a commercial product—that was the holographic logic chip manufacturing facility.

There had been several false starts into the market place by Megatric. Most of the money that the division made was from government research grants. There were many activities going on at the company that seemed to Laz to be useless. He consentrated on the sales of Megatric's holographic logic chip. As a matter of fact, W.T. Technologies was one of Megatric's customers. This allowed Laz the excuse of seeing I.C. Whiz at W.T. Technologies "on official business." The holographic world, after all, was a small one.

Lazarus Time spent about 20 hours a week at W.T. Technologies and billed the company every week for his services. An accountant friend of his told him that it was a good time for him to start learning about accounting. Since the income he was getting from W.T. was considered business income, he had to start keeping track of his related expenses.

Furthermore, Ignatz wasn't too good at accounting, so Laz knew that he would eventually have to understand accounting at W.T.

To Lazarus accounting was just another subject that he had to master. Lazarus signed up at the local university extension night class and began going every Wednesday night to school. The course was entitled "Understanding Accounting ISX 124512."

The first night Lax came to class he saw at the front of the room a man with curly long hair and pants that were too long. The cuffs of the instructor's pants came over his shoes and every time he walked, he stepped on the cuffs of his pants.

After the customary opening remarks and class introduction, the instructor with the long pants took a deep breath and started to explain accounting. . . .

THE ACCOUNTING SYSTEM IN BALANCE AND TRANSFORMATION

All accounts used by a business can be grouped under the six major headings: assets, liabilities, equity, income, expenses, and cost of sales. Let's discuss them one at a time.

Assets

Assets are what a business owns. An asset is property that is used in a trade or business. This property contributes toward earning the income of the business, whether directly or indirectly. Assets are productive items which contribute to income. Assets are tangible property, promises of future receipt of cash (such as accounts receivable), or investments made in the business that are not considered.

The committee on terminology of the American Institute of Certified Public Accountants (AICPA), in its *Accounting Terminology Bulletin No. 1* defined asset as follows:

The word *asset* is not synonymous with or limited to property but includes also that part of any cost of expense incurred which is properly carried forward upon a closing of books at a specific date. [An asset] represents whether a property right or value acquired, or an expenditure made, which has created a property right, is properly applicable to the future. Thus plant, accounts receivable, inventory, and a deferred charge are all assets.

Assets include the following items (accounts):

- Cash
- Accounts receivable
- Inventory
- Investments
- Prepaid expense (such as last month's rent or utility deposits)
- Equipment
- Motor vehicles
- Furniture and fixtures
- Land and buildings
- Building improvements (or leasehold improvements if you are a renter)
- Other tangible property
- Goodwill
- Patents and copyrights
- Organizational expense
- Research and development

All these items can be divided into three categories, current, fixed, and other assets.

Current assets are those items that can be readily converted into cash within a one year period. They are assets in which the flow of funds is one of continuous circulation or turnover in the short run. *Fixed assets* are items of property, plant, and equipment referred to as "fixed" because of their permanent nature and because they are not subject to rapid turnover. Fixed assets are used in connection with producing or earning revenue and are not for sale in the ordinary course of business. *Other assets* are all the assets that are not current and cannot fit into the fixed asset category (such as research and development or goodwill) (see figure 2.1).

Current Assets
Cash
Accounts receivable
Inventory
Short-term investments

Fixed Assets
Equipment
Motor vehicles
Furniture and fixtures
Land and buildings
Building improvements (or leasehold improvements)

Other Assets
Prepaid expense
Goodwill
Patents and copyrights
Organizational expense
Research and development

Figure 2.1   Assets.

Liabilities

Liabilities are what a business owes to others. Liabilities include debts of the company—amounts of money owed but not yet paid.
   Liabilities include the following items (accounts):

- Accounts payable (money owed for inventory, outside labor, etc.)
- Notes payable (the notes, usually secured by some asset or personal guarantee, that require repayment, such as bank debt or mortgages.)
- Accrued expenses (like income tax payable, salaries payable, rent payable—amounts that you now owe but haven't paid).
- Trade payables (generally called accounts payable)
- Provision for pensions
- Bonds
- Debentures

Liabilities are generally considered to be either current or long-term. Current liabilities are those debts existing as of the balance sheet date which are due for payment within one year or within the normal operating cycle of the business. Long-term, or fixed, liabilities are those debts that will be paid in a period longer than one year (see Figure 2.2).

Owners' Equity

Owners' equity or capital is the owners' claim to funds invested in the business and the earnings kept in the business over the years. In a sole proprietorship (business owned by one person), owner's equity is shown as a single balance sheet figure covering both the capital an owner has put into the business and the net earnings left there. In a partnership, the owner's equity is usually shown on the balance sheet classified by individual partners. In a corporation, the owners' equity is shown in a

Equities: Liabilities
Current liabilities
   Accounts payable
   Notes payable (one year portion)
   Accrued expense
   Bonds [current (one year) portion]
   Debentures (current portion)

Long-term liabilities
   Notes payable—amount due after one year
   Bonds—amount due after one year
   Debentures—amount due after one year

Equities: Owner's Capital
In a sole proprietorship
   Net worth

In a partnership
   Net worth—one partner
   Net worth—another partner

In a corporation
   Capital stock
   Retained earnings

Figure 2.2

balance sheet in at least two parts: (1) capital stock (or paid-in capital) and (2) retained earnings. The capital stock is shown at "par" or "stated value." The difference between the par value and the amount paid initially for the stock by the stockholders, less costs, is shown as "paid-in surplus" (see Figure 2.2).

Owners' equity can be shown as:

- For sole proprietorships or partnerships—equity, entered as one line on the balance sheet.
- For corporations—capital stock, paid-in surplus, and retained earnings.

Income

Income (or revenue) is the amounts that a business receives for its goods and services. For the majority of companies—those that sell on credit—sales means the amount of goods shipped during a given accounting period. Sales may be extended to cover fees for services performed as well as other items of income such as commissions, rents, and royalties.

For sales involving the shipment of goods, there is normally a passing of legal title, which is evidence that a sale has in fact taken place. In other types of business transactions revenue recognition is not dependent on the passing of title. For example, service industries do not pass legal title when they perform a service for their customers.

Income usually includes the following items (accounts):

- Merchandise sales
- Rental income

- Commissions
- Royalties
- Fees for services

Operating Expense

Operating expenses are the costs of operating a business that are not the direct cost of sales. Operating expenses include all overhead costs such as salaries and rent as well as the expenses of selling the product of service. Direct costs required to produce sales such as inventory costs or manufacturing costs are considered "cost of sales." Expenses are period costs and not inventory costs. Operating expenses are the costs to operate a business and are more or less independent of the sales level.

Expenses include the following items (accounts):

- Wages and salaries
- Rental expense (including equipment or premise leases).
- Repairs
- Replacements
- Depreciation
- Bad debt
- Travel and transportation
- Business entertainment
- Interest expense (on debt repayment)
- Insurance
- Taxes (payroll, social security, personal property, real property)
- Office supplies
- Accounting and legal expense
- Utilities (heat, gas, electric, telephone, etc.)
- Advertising
- Licenses and regulatory fees
- Charitable contributions
- Donations to business organizations and industry associations
- Commitment fees or standby charges you incur in a mortgaging agreement
- Freight and postage

Cost of Sales

Cost of sales, sometimes considered to be an operating expense, is the cost of the merchandise sold. It does not cover the expenses of selling or shipping this merchandise or, ordinarily, any storing, office, or general administrative expenses involved in company operations. These items are considered operating expense.

In professional and service businesses, there is usually no cost of sales because these companies receive income from fees, rents, and the like, and not from the sale of inventories.

In businesses that have inventories, such as retail, wholesale, and manufacturing businesses, there is a cost of sales.

Income
Merchandise sales
Rental income
Commissions
Royalties
Fees for services

Operating Expenses
Wages and salaries
Rent
Repairs
Replacements
Depreciation
Bad debt
Travel and transportation
Entertainment
Interest
Insurance
Taxes
Office and other supplies
Accounting and legal
Utilities
Advertising
Licenses and fees
Donations
Freight and postage
Commitment fees

Figure 2.3   Determinates of net profit.

Net profit is determined by subtracting total expenses and cost of sales from income (see Figure 2.3).

THE BASIC ACCOUNTING EQUATION AND PERMANENT AND TEMPORARY ACCOUNTS

The basic accounting equation, the formula from which all accounting logic proceeds, is:

Assets = Liabilities + Equity (owner's capital)

Using the rules of algebra, this can also be stated as:

Assets − liabilities = equity,
or
Assets − equity = liabilities,
or
Assets − equity − liabilities = 0 (zero)

In other words, the total dollar amount of assets equals the total dollar amount of equity plus liabilities. The dollar amount of assets minus the dollar amount of liabilities (or equity) equals the total dollar amount of equity (or liabilities). If you subtract the total dollar volume of liabilities and capital from assets, you get zero.

Both sides of the equation are in *balance*, the total of one side (assets) equals the total of the other side (liabilities plus equity). When these three accounts are put in document form, that document is called a *balance sheet*, one of the basic documents of accounting.

The equation means that the value of the properties a business owns (assets) are equal to the value of the rights in those properties (liabilities and equity). Liabilities are the creditors' (banks, trade, etc.) rights in the business. Equity is the owners' rights in the business. So rights in properties equal the amount of properties.

Income, Expense, and Cost of Sales

We have talked about the three of the six groups of accounts: assets, liabilities, and equity. So what about the other three groups of accounts: income, expense, and cost of sales? Income, cost of sales, and expense make up a second fundamental accounting document called an income statement or *profit and loss statement* (P&L for short). The income statement takes the sales (income) for a period and reduces it by cost of sales and expenses, resulting in a *net profit*. This net profit, after such cash costs as loan principal reduction, taxes, and dividends or draw, is posted to the equity account as *retained earnings*. This process can be illustrated as follows:

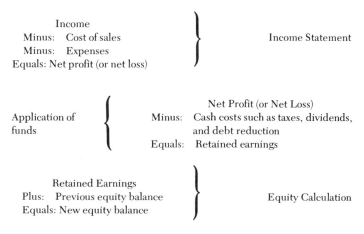

Income
Minus: Cost of sales
Minus: Expenses
Equals: Net profit (or net loss)
} Income Statement

Application of funds {
Net Profit (or Net Loss)
Minus: Cash costs such as taxes, dividends, and debt reduction
Equals: Retained earnings

Retained Earnings
Plus: Previous equity balance
Equals: New equity balance
} Equity Calculation

So, income, cost of sales, and expense are in effect part of the equity account; the result of taking income and subtracting cost of sales, expenses, and dividends in either an increase (caused by net profit) or a decrease (caused by net loss) in the equity account.

Income, cost of sales, and expenses fit into the basic accounting equation of *Assets = Liabilities + Equity* by being part of the equity account.

Let's expand the basic accounting equation to include income, expense, and cost of sales. The equation can be restated:

assets = liabilities + previous equity + income − cost of sales − costs (costs include expense and cash costs—taxes, draw, etc).

The only way that a business grows is by making money (profit after costs). If the business makes money, the worth (net worth or equity) of business is greater. If a company loses money, the worth of the company (equity) is less. The net cash that a company makes is the money that an owner has available from the business; it's the owner's equity.

The income, expense, and cost of sales accounts are a part of the equity account, but only a temporary part. Income less cost of sales less expense is only posted to equity *once* per period. If the accounting period for a business is one year, the income statement accounts (income, expense, and cost of sales) only become incorporated into equity once per year. This makes sense because it would be much too troublesome to incorporate these three large groups of accounts into the equity account constantly. This would cause the equity account to have a larger number of entries than the cash account. In short, it is accounting convention to incorporate income, cost of sales, and expense into equity no more than once per accounting period (month, quarter, year).

When income, cost of sales, and expense (the income statement accounts) are *posted* (or put as part of equity), the separate accounts are zeroed out. All the entries in the income statement accounts are made zero and they start out as zero in the account to begin the next period.

The following is an example of an end of the period journal entry, closing various income and expense accounts to the income and expense summary, an equity account:

Date	Explanation	Debit	Credit
12/31/78	Income	$150,000	
	Income and expense summary		$150,000
	Income and expense summary	142,000	
	Merchandise purchases		120,000
	Salary expense		10,000
	Rental expense		4,000
	Utilities		2,000
	Supplies		1,000
	Taxes		500
	Accounting		1,200
	Entertainment		2,300
	Transportation and travel		1,000
	To record transfer of accounts to income and expense summary.		

The following shows how the salary expense *ledger* account is zeroed out by the above journal entries:

Date	Explanation	Debit	Credit
1/30/80	CDJ—2*	$ 1,000	
6/30/80	CDJ—10	1,000	
12/31/80	CDJ—21	1,000	
	Total	12,000	
12/31/80	GJ—12—3†		$12,000

Income, expense, and cost of sales accounts are zeroed out and closed once per period. Therefore they are considered *temporary* accounts.

Assets, liabilities, and equity (to which the temporary accounts are closed once per period) are considered *permanent* accounts because they are never closed or zeroed out at the end of a period. These accounts are the basic accounts of the business and the only time they will be zero is if they are physically reduced by some event such as selling off an asset, spending all the cash then in the bank, paying off a debt, or taking all the money out of equity.

If all the assets are sold and all the asset accounts are reduced to zero, the business ceases to exist. If all the equity account equals zero, the business has as much debt as assets and the business is in trouble. If there is zero debt (no liabilities), the company would be considered unusual. This circumstance generally exists only when a business is just starting. In short, it is a rare instance when any of the three account groups, (assets, liabilities, and equity) are zero.

*CDJ stands for cash disbursements journal, the journal these entries came from. The number after the CDJ is the page number of the cash disbursements journal that the entry was posted from.

†GJ means general journal. The number after GJ is the absolute number of the entry illustrated in the journal entry just above. General journal entries are usually numbered sequentially—the first number (12) stands for the month of the entry and the second number (3) is the number of the general journal entry that month, taken sequentially.

Assets, liabilities, and equity are permanent accounts that generally cease to exist only when the business ceases to exist.

Thus we can understand. . .

The class instructor looked at his watch and stopped in mid-sentence. "Next week," he said, "we will talk about original accounting documents. These original documents include things like cash register receipts, invoices, and so on. The IRS requires these original documents although they do not require books.

"What it boils down to," the instructor ran his fingers through his curly hair and transferred the chalk dust on his hands to his head (as the class progressed, the instructor's hair always became whiter and whiter). "What it boils down to is that if you learn nothing else about accounting, you should learn about original documents. Remember, next week is excitement time. See you then."

Lazarus Time walked back to his car going over the salient points: assets equal liabilities and net worth. There are only six account groups in accounting: assets, liabilities, equity of the owner, income, expense, and cost of sales. Assets, liabilities, and equity are permanent accounts—they are *never* closed and opened again. Income, cost of sales, and expenses are temporary accounts. They *end* when the year ends; then they are started over again with zero balance.

As he got into his car Laz noticed that the instructor was at the other end of the parking lot using a coat hanger to try to get into his car. "He must have lost his key," Laz said. But the instructor seemed to be doing okay so Laz drove home.

Chapter Three
Original Transaction Documents

What a day it had been for Lazarus Time. He had lunch with his partner, Ignatz Whiz. Ignatz told him that their company, W.T. Technologies, was in serious trouble. They hadn't had any orders in over a month, salaries had to be met, and W.T. Technologies' bank account was already overdrawn. But that wasn't all. . . .

That morning Laz had been told that the only commercial holographic product at Megatric was in serious trouble because of scheduling.

All this and he hadn't seen his girlfriend or a living soul outside of business in almost four days. And now he was driving to a night class in accounting.

Laz didn't exactly understand how he felt. He felt queasy and weak. He felt like he was getting sick. But it wasn't a stomach-ache. It wasn't a headache. He was looking out at the world as if through a haze.

He was in his car and heading for the extension class, but Laz felt like seeing his girlfriend instead. Forget the class, forget the mess that the day had been.

But he knew why he was sick. He had problems and now he had to face them. While waiting for the instructor to come into the class, Laz pulled out some paper and started making sketches on it. "Maybe a systems approach with these problems," he thought, "would work."

The instructor was about 15 minutes late and people in the class started getting nervous. They thought he might be sick. Just then the instructor came huffing into class, his shirt collar sticking stright up in the air and his tie askew. "I'm sorry I'm late," the instructor told the class. "I had a flat tire on the highway." The instructor's shirt tails were hanging out over the back of his pants. His shirt had black tire-dust smudges on it.

"What was I going to talk about tonight?" The instructor looked at his notes, "Oh, yeah. Important stuff, the. . ."

ORIGINAL TRANSACTION DOCUMENTS

The first step for accountants of today is the same as it was for an accountant of 5000 years ago. They must record and understand the original transaction documents. The original transaction documents are those documents such as fee billings, cash register receipts, checks, shipping documents, invoices, petty cash slips, deposit slips, and so on that represent the first recording of a business transaction at the point of exchange.

We will consider these original transaction documents in the order of their common use. The documents can be grouped as follows:

- Sales documents (bill to client)
- Bank documents (check, check register, deposit slips)
- Petty cash
- Purchasing documents
- Shipping and invoice documents
- Travel and entertainment records
- Payroll records

Bank Documents

The most commonly used bank documents are the *check* and the *deposit slip* (illustrated in Figures 3.1 and 3.2). Checks and deposit slips are usually coded at the bottom with the account number of the business so that they can be read by automated equipment. The name of the business and the address is usually printed in the top left-hand corner. The check has spaces for the date, the payee (person to whom the check is made out), a signature, and usually a comment space. The deposit slip lists all the currency, coin and/or checks to be deposited. Checks are listed separately with a code located on the top part of the fraction in the upper right-hand corner of a check. The amounts are totaled.

Whenever a check is written by a company, it is recorded on a *check stub* or *check register*. In the check register (Figure 3.3) the amount of each check, date, check number, payee, and account number or explanation are recorded each time a check is written. The check register may also have a space for entering deposits. Deposits are recorded by date, who from, reason, and total.

Note. When depositing checks two types of endorsements may be used. One endorsement is simply the signature of the payee. The other is the "restrictive endorsement." This is an endorsement that indicates the check is for deposit only before the signature. Figure 3.1 illustrates a restrictive endorsement.

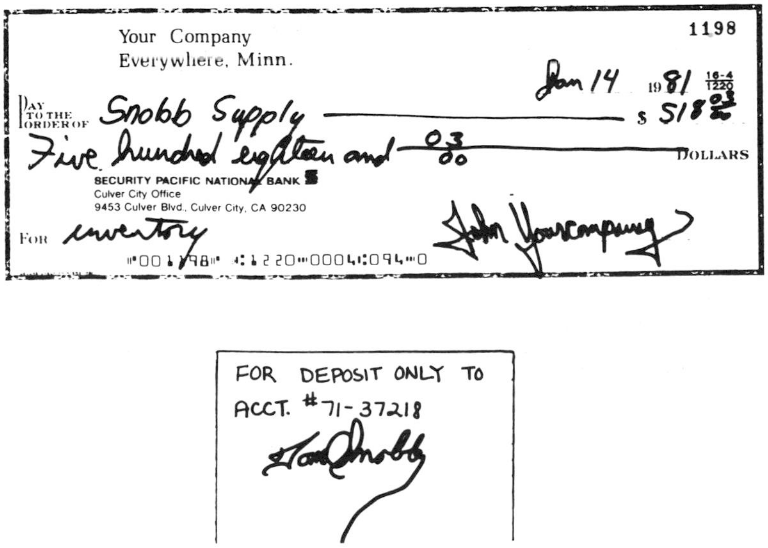

Figure 3.1

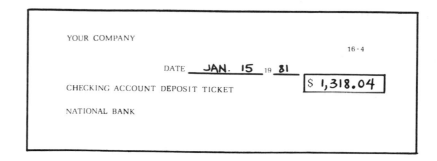

YOUR COMPANY

16-4

DATE __JAN. 15__ 19 __81__

CHECKING ACCOUNT DEPOSIT TICKET

$ 1,318.04

NATIONAL BANK

	CHECKS	DOLLARS	CENTS
1	16-20	412	01
2	4-18	310	73
3	6-71	242	12
4			

35			
36			
Checks		964	86
Currency		321	00
Coin		32	18
TOTAL		1,318	04

Figure 3.2

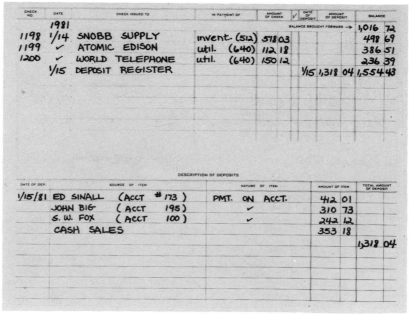

CHECK NO.	DATE	CHECK ISSUED TO	IN PAYMENT OF	AMOUNT OF CHECK	✓	DATE OF DEPOSIT	AMOUNT OF DEPOSIT	BALANCE
	1981					BALANCE BROUGHT FORWARD →		1,016 72
1198	1/14	SNOBB SUPPLY	invent. (512)	518 03				498 69
1199	✓	ATOMIC EDISON	util. (640)	112 18				386 51
1200	✓	WORLD TELEPHONE	util. (640)	150 12				236 39
	1/15	DEPOSIT REGISTER				1/15	1,318 04	1,554 43

DESCRIPTION OF DEPOSITS

DATE OF DEP.	SOURCE OF ITEM	NATURE OF ITEM	AMOUNT OF ITEM	TOTAL AMOUNT OF DEPOSIT
1/15/81	ED SINALL (ACCT #173)	PMT. ON ACCT.	412 01	
	JOHN BIG (ACCT 195)	✓	310 73	
	S. W. FOX (ACCT 100)	✓	242 12	
	CASH SALES		353 18	
				1,318 04

Figure 3.3

Other bank documents include savings account deposit slips and withdrawal slips (a deposit slip is illustrated in Figure 3.4). Savings account slips require the name of the depositer, account number, date, and total deposited or withdrawn.

Petty Cash

Most businesses set aside a small sum of cash for the payment of minor business expenses. This sum of cash is called the "petty cash fund" and it is either kept in a cash box or envelope. Items that are usually paid out of petty cash include postage, transportation, telegrams, incidental office supplies, and sometimes parking duplicating, and entertainment expense (for lunches, etc.).

Figure 3.5 illustrates a petty cash envelope or *office fund voucher* as it is called in the illustration. When money is paid out of petty cash the receipt is placed in the envelope and a notation is made indicating the date, the receipt number (if any), to whom it was paid, what expense category it falls under, the account number and the amount. At the bottom of the envelope in our illustration there are columns for recording the "distribution" of the expenses to the different accounts. The first entry on the cash voucher envelope in the example is for postage expense—$3.50 paid to the U.S. Post Office on January 5, 1980. A notation is made that the postage account is account 510. At the bottom of the envelope the two entries recorded for postage are entered in a column under account 510.

Purchasing Documents

Sometimes a business can simply order supplies by telephone, but many suppliers will require it to request merchandise by written order. The form for requesting goods is called a *purchase order*, and is sent by the purchaser to the company that will supply the goods. Purchase orders are usually in triplicate, with each copy in a different color. One copy is sent to the vendor (supplier), the second copy is usually retained for the purchasing company files, and the third copy is furnished to the receiving department where the goods are to be delivered.

The purchase order usually contains the following information.

- Number of the purchase order
- Name and address of the vendor
- Name and address where the goods are to be shipped

Figure 3.4

OFFICE FUND VOUCHER   No. ___1___

From ___1 JAN___ 19 _80_ to _____ 19___ Paid by Check No. _____

AUDITED BY		APPROVED BY			

DATE	RECEIPT NO.	TO WHOM PAID	FOR WHAT	ACCOUNT	AMOUNT
1/5/80		U.S. POST OFFICE	POSTAGE	510	3 50
1/7/80		COPY CROP	DUPLICATING	.511	20 16
1/10/80		DOWN TOWN PARKING	PARKING	512	2 50
1/15/80		COPY CROP	DUPLICATING	511	7 40
1/20/80		U.S. POST OFFICE	POSTAGE	510	7 50
1/22/80		GREEN ONION	DINNER - C. ZAP	520	14 80
			TOTAL DISBURSED		
			CASH ON HAND		
			AMOUNT OF FUND		

Post.	Dupl.	Park.	Ent.	**DISTRIBUTION**					
510	511	512	520						
3 50	20 16	2 50	14 80						
7 50	7 40								

Figure 3.5

- Special shipping instructions
- Date
- Quantity, description, and price of the items ordered

The vendor prepares an invoice, or bill to send to the buyer when he ships the goods (illustrated in Figure 3.6).

When these invoices are packed with the shipment, they are referred to as *packing slips*. The vendor may also mail the invoice directly to the buyer. This invoice transfers rights to property, providing the property is paid for, to the buyer.

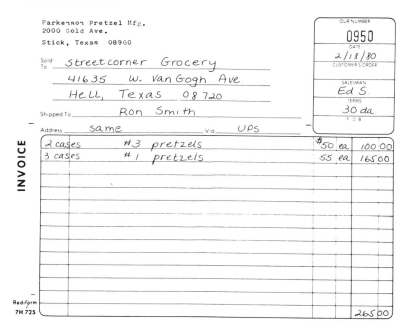

Figure 3.6

Travel and Entertainment Records

The Securities and Exchange Commission (SEC) requirement passed in 1977 that businesses disclose "perks" (perquisites) given to employees that were previously considered company-paid entertainment and travel expense. Pending IRS regulations, this has caused a confusion about what constitutes legal travel and entertainment expense.

Figure 3.7 is an illustration of an expense report for travel and entertainment. It breaks down the cost for 11 separate items, one of which is not tax deductible as an expense. The items recorded are:

1. *Transportation* — airfare, trainfare, busfare, or transportation by automobile compensated at some rate per mile. Note that part of the way down the page this item is broken into destination and departure points. Receipts should be included if the amount of this transportation cost is over $25.00, but it is wisest to include receipts no matter what the cost.

2. *Taxi-limousine-carfare* — the cost of transportation by private or public transport at the destination or departure points. This is also broken down by departure and destination.

3. *Hotel* — the cost of room at a hotel. Receipts are always required.

4. *Meals–personal* — not deductible.

5. *Telephone-telegraph* — business related communication costs. Whenever possible receipts should be kept for this, too.

6. *Laundry-valet service* — laundry costs required by business necessities.

7. *Other auto* — the cost of tools, parking, service, repairs, and the like. Receipts should be kept. These are itemized in a section at the bottom of the report.

8. *Tips.*

EXPENSE REPORT FOR RECORDING I.R.S. DATA

NAME: JOHN T. SNOBB	TERR. OR DEPT.: SALES MGR.	DATE OF REPORT: 1/30/80

PURPOSE OF TRIP: SALE / EMERSON ACCOUNT	DATE OF TRIP FROM 1/23/80 TO 1/27/80

ITEM	EXPENSE	SUN. / /	MON. 1/23/80	TUES. 1/24/80	WED. 1/25/80	THUR. 1/26/80	FRI. 1/27/80	SAT. / /	ITEM TOTALS
* 1	TRANSPORTATION ($25. OR OVER) (ATT. RECEIPT)		150 00				150 00		300 00
* 2	TAXI·LIMOUSINE·CARFARE		9 50	20 10	6 30	4 20	3 -		43 10
3	HOTEL (ATTACH RECEIPT)		18 -	18 -	18 -	18 -	18 -		72 00
4	MEALS (PERSONAL USE ONLY) (NO. 11 FOR OTHER)		2 16		3 38	4 15	1 26		10 95
5	TELEPHONE · TELEGRAM			3 50	2 -	4 -			9 50
6	LAUNDRY · VALET SERVICE								
* 7	OTHER AUTO PARKING·TOLLS SERVICE·REPAIRS								
8	TIPS · CHECKING · OTHER		2 -	1 50	3 -	2 -	6 -		14 50
9	POSTAGE		3 50	75					
* 10	MISCELLANEOUS & GIFTS								33 03
* 11	ENTERTAINMENT			26 38	6 65				
	DAILY TOTALS ⟶		185 16	70 23	39 33	32 35	160 26		487 33

NON·REIMBURSED EXPENDITURES (PERSONAL RECORD)		ACCOUNTING	AMT. ADVANCE
SUN.		REMARKS:	$ 400 -
MON.	2 16		EXP. ABOVE
TUES.			
WED.	3 38		$ 476.38
THU.	4 15		DIFFERENCE
FRI.	1 26	CHECKED BY:	
SAT.		APPROVED BY:	$ 76.38
TOTAL	10 95	DATE:	

* EXPLAIN BELOW IN DETAIL

ITEM		SUN.	MON.	TUE.	WED.	THUR.	FRI.	SAT.
1	FROM		L.A.X.				Geo., Fla.	
	TO		Geo, Fla.				L.A.X.	
	TO							
	TO							
	AUTO MILEAGE							
2	FROM		Airport	hotel	hotel	hotel	hotel	
	TO		Hotel	downtown	city hall	indust prk	airport	
	FROM		hotel	downtown	city hall	indust prk		
	TO		downtown	indust. prk	hotel	hotel		
	FROM		downtown	indust. prk				
	TO		hotel	hotel				

ITEM	DATE	AUTO·PARKING·TOLLS·SERVICE·REPAIRS	AMOUNT	ITEM	DATE	ENTERTAINMENT·SHOW CUSTOMER NAME & TITLE AMT. PLACE & BUSINESS PUR. POSE $25 OR OVER ATT. RECPT	AMOUNT
7				11	1/24	T. Biggs, Genl Mgr. Emerson mfg., Tony's Pizza, discuss purchase of new equip	6 13
10		MISC.·SHOW NAME, COST, PURPOSE $25. OR OVER ATT. RECEIPT			1/24	J. Emerson, Pres. Emerson mfg. La Ritz, negotiate new purchase	20 25
					1/25	T. Biggs, J. Emerson, drinks Corner Grill, finalize sale	6 65

SIGNED X *John T. Snobb*	APPROVED BY X	DATE / /

PART 1 WITH RECEIPTS ATTACHED TO APPROPRIATE OFFICE
Rediform ® 9H976

PAI · RETAINED AS YOUR RECORD OF EXPENSE

Figure 3.7

9. *Postage*—for business correspondence.

10. *Miscellaneous and gifts*—carefully itemized as to name of receipient, cost, and purpose. Gifts cannot be for more than $25 per person per year.

11. *Entertainment expense*—requires careful attention to reporting details. In addition to the breakdown at the bottom of the report, the authors suggest that you attach receipts and give particulars as to customer's name and title, place of business, amount, and what was discussed. We would suggest that the reporter maintain at least one paragraph summaries of what was discussed at each meeting.

If there are further tax restrictions on expense, entertainment expense is the area where it will most likely occur. But as long as entertainment expense was incurred for business purposes and this was carefully documented, the businessperson has little to worry about.

"Break time," the instructor said, and headed out the door for the snack shop downstairs.

Lazarus Time stayed at his desk. While the instructor was talking, Laz had devised a plan for helping out W.T. Technologies. The procedure would be:

- Borrow some short-term money to cover the payroll.
- Try to get some stop-gap sales—by dropping the price if necessary.
- Devise a long-range sales and production plan.

Lazarus looked at these three points and tried to reason them out. Yes, it seemed like a good plan.

How about the productivity and scheduling of the holographic logic chip at Megatric? Selling the thing wasn't difficult. The logic chip was back-ordered for three months, but the customers were getting uneasy. The company was supposed to produce 1000 units per month but for some reason they had never produced more than 500 and in the last two months production has been slumping.

Laz was a marketing man. He had never had much production experience. But it was becoming apparent that he could no longer sit around and let the plant supervisor handle this. He had to get into the act or his customers would start canceling orders.

The instructor began talking: "Payroll taxes and payroll tax records always seem to confuse people. I hope what we talk about tonight will help some of you. . . ."

Payroll Records

If you have any employees in your business, you have certain obligations to the federal government for payment of payroll taxes and withholding of income taxes. You will probably have similar obligations for payroll and/or withholding taxes to state or local governments.

Federal regulations do not prescribe the form in which your payroll records must be kept, but the records should include the following information and documents:

1. The amounts and dates of all wage payments subject to withholding taxes and the amounts withheld.
2. The names, addresses, and occupations of employees receiving payments.
3. The periods of their employment.
4. The periods for which they are paid by you while they are absent because of sickness or personal injuries, and the amount and weekly rate of payments.
5. Their social security account numbers if they are subject to social security tax.
6. Their income tax withholding exemption certificates.
7. Your employer identifcation number.
8. Duplicate copies of returns filed.
9. Dates and amounts of deposits made with government.

Usually, an employee's earnings card is set up for each employee. Every wage payment to the employee is recorded on this card, along with all the information needed for meeting federal, state, and city requirements relating to payroll and withholding taxes, and all other amounts deducted from the employee's wages.

A number of payroll-records systems are available commercially. Most of these are based on the pegborad or multiple-copy principle. A single writing of a check or payslip to be given to the employee makes a carbon entry on the employee's earnings card and on a payroll summary or journal for each pay period. If you have only one or two employees, it is usually not necessary to have a special payroll system. Paychecks may be entered directly in your cash disbursements journal or on an earnings card for each employee. Figure 3.8 illustrates two payroll records.

There are three types of federal payroll taxes: (1) income taxes withheld, (2) social security taxes, and (3) federal unemployment taxes. IRS *Publication 15*, "Employer's Tax Guide," should be consulted for additional information about employer-employee relationships, what constitutes taxable wages, the treatment of special types of employment and payments, and similar matters.

Income taxes are withheld on all wages paid an employee above a certain minimum. The minimum is governed by the number of exemptions claimed by an employee. The Tax Reduction and Simplification Act of 1977 changed the standard deduction to a flat rate of $2200 for single individuals and $3200 for married couples filing joint returns.

EMPLOYER

EMP. NO. 318-92-8550   PAY FOR PERIOD ENDING   1/7/80

EMPLOYEE'S NAME   JoAnne Topps

DATE HIRED   1/1   DATE DISCHARGED
PLACE OF EMPLOYMENT   SCHEDULE HOURS THIS PERIOD

DAYS AND HOURS WORKED

	SUN.	MON.	TUES.	WED.	THURS.	FRI.	SAT.	TOTAL DAYS	TOTAL HOURS	RATE PER HR.		
HOURS		8	8	8	8	8		5	40	5.00		
OVER TIME												

SALARY (If paid on fixed Weekly or Monthly Basis)

REMUNERATION OTHER THAN CASH (Room, Board, Tips, etc.)

GROSS EARNINGS	200	00
DEDUCTIONS		
% WITHHOLDING TAX Table	21	40
1 % STATE DISABILITY INSURANCE	2	00
6.05 % FED. INS. CONTRIBUTION ACT	12	40
% STATE WITHHOLDING TAX	5	70
TOTAL DEDUCTIONS	41	50
NET EARNINGS	158	50

LESS: REMUNERATION OTHER THAN CASH

☐ BY CASH
☒ BY CHECK NO. 138   NET PAY THIS PERIOD 158 50

I HEREBY CERTIFY THAT THE TIME SHOWN ABOVE IS CORRECT
EMPLOYEE SIGN HERE   JoAnne Topps

4H417 Rediform ®

Figure 3.8

Social security taxes apply to the first $25,000 (in 1980) of wages paid an employee during a year. A percentage deduction (presently 6.5%) from the employee's wages is matched by an *equal amount* in taxes paid by the employer.

In addition to taxes withheld from employees' salaries and also paid by the employer, there is another tax that is paid by the employer *only*. This is the federal unemployment tax (FUTA), which is required only of employers who have (1) paid wages of $1500 or more in any calendar quarter (2) employed one or more persons for some portion of at least one day during each of 20 different calendar weeks. The 20 weeks do not have to be consecutive. Individuals on vacation or sick leave are counted as employees in determining the business's status. After 1977, the taxation rate is 3.4% on the first $6000 of wages paid to each employee.

If you are required to withhold income tax from wages or are liable for social security taxes in excess of $200 quarterly, you must file a quarterly return, Form 941. Form 941 combines the social security taxes (including hospital insurance) and income tax withholding. Form 941E is used for reporting income tax withheld from wages, tips, annuities, and supplemental unemployment compensation benefits when no FICA coverage is required.

Due dates for the Forms 941 or 941E and the full payment of tax are as follows:

Quarter	Due dates
January–February–March	April 30
April–May–June	July 31
July–August–September	October 31
October–November–December	January 31, next year

If you are required to make deposits of taxes and you make timely deposits in full payment of the taxes due, you may file your quarterly return on or before the 10th day of the second month following the period for which it is made. In this case the due dates are as follows:

Quarter	Due dates
January–February–March	May 10
April–May–June	August 10
July–August–September	November 10
October–November–December	February 10, next year

Deposits are made by completing and filing Form 501, "Federal Tax Deposit," together with a single remittance covering the taxes to be deposited to an authorized commercial bank or federal reserve bank in accordance with instructions on the form. Names of authorized commercial bank depositories are available at your local bank.

Lazarus Time headed toward his automobile with two commitments for the next day. First he would talk to the bank about a loan for W.T. Technologies. Then he would go down to the logic chip plant and see what was causing production to lag.

The cold, damp air hit his face through the open windows of his moving car. He felt good.

Chapter Four
The Books

It was 10:00 A.M. and Lazarus Time was standing in front of the Silicon Valley branch of Bank Amerigold. He had called the branch manager and arranged an early meeting to discuss the chances of W.T. Technologies getting financing.

When a guard opened the door a whole herd of people came streaming into the bank. Laz had never met anyone at the bank. He was supposed to see Mr. Pumiceheart about the loan. He looked around and saw a balding man in his forties behind a desk in the middle of the floor. The brass plate on the desk said, "Ronald Pumiceheart, Assistant Vice President." Mr. Pumiceheart was not smiling.

Laz walked up to the desk and the man said in a critical tone, "Can I help you?"

"Are you Mr. Pumiceheart?"

"Yes."

"I talked with you this morning about a loan. My name is Lazarus Time. My company is W.T. Technologies. We manufacture holographic memories." Laz sat down as Mr. Pumiceheart gestured with his hand.

"How much do you want?" Mr. Pumice asked as he shuffled through some papers on his desk and pulled out a legal-sized yellow sheet.

"We are in need of some working capital." Laz said.

"How much?" Mr. Pumiceheart pursued.

"Around thirty thousand should do." Laz said hesitantly.

"For how long?"

"Well, we should be able to be in a position to repay the loan in three months."

"You need a short-term loan then?" Mr. Pumiceheart asked.

"Yeah."

"You want the money for working capital. What would you do with the money?" Pumiceheart had not looked up from his yellow pad yet.

Laz was hesitant. He didn't know whether he should tell the banker that they didn't have any income and they needed the money to keep their heads above water. "Well, we started the business with our own money. The business is having a little slump in sales now and we needed a loan to get us producing while sales are increasing." Mr. Pumiceheart asked, "How long have you been in this business?"

"About seven months." Laz answered.

"Do you have financial statements? Have you had an accountant prepare these statements?"

"No." Laz didn't know what else to say, and he was pretty damn nervous about a loan.

"It might be a good idea to talk to him. I need financial statements for the end of last month. When you get the financial statements, please come back and we'll talk again." Mr. Pumiceheart pulled a folder from the drawer of his desk while ripping the top page of the yellow note pad off. He put the yellow page in the folder. He then sat there with his hands folded looking at Lazarus.

A long period of silence followed.

Lazarus jumped up quickly, and "Ah, goodbye. I'll do that. I'll get an accountant." He shook hands and left the bank.

As he drove to Megatric he had to keep talking to himself out loud to calm the queasiness he had in his stomach. "Well," he told himself, "this accounting stuff appears to be more important than I thought. The bank can't even *talk* to me about a loan without it. I'm going to have to get an accountant. W.T. Technologies hasn't even kept any regular books."

No one at the company knew anything about accounting. They kept their check register up to date. They had all their original transaction documents such as bills of sale, salary slips, shipping slips, and the like. But these were all in folders and boxes. "What did the instructor at university extension say?" Lazarus again spoke out loud. "The IRS doesn't require books, the instructor said. Well, *banks* do."

When he arrived at the office, Laz telephoned his ex-brother-in-law. Laz hadn't spoken to him in five years. He felt embarrassed calling and asking for a favor. But this seemed the only solution to his present predicament. After a brief conversation, his ex-brother-in-law gave Laz the name of a CPA he knew—Pete Popstein.

Lazarus called Popstein and set up an appointment at W.T. Technologies. Lazarus had been keeping receipts for the consulting he did for W.T. Technologies. He thought that since Popstein would come to explain and assist with set up the books, he might as well have the books set up for his consulting venture at the same time.

Until the meeting with the accountant, Laz had his hands full trying to get sales for W.T. Technologies and trying to watch the scheduling at Megatric's Holographic Memory division.

The day of the meeting with Popstein arrived and Lazarus and Ignatz Whiz were ready. They had all the original documents that Popstein has asked for and they had purchased in advance a set of blank books—one called a *journal* and one called a *ledger*.

Pete Popstein was a round man with a very youthful face. He had curly brown hair and a pinkish-white complexion. He had six pens and pencils in his right shirt pocket, clipped to a plastic shirt protector.

Pete looked at the materials they had and asked them a few questions. "Okay," he said, "I understand that what you want is for me to tell you a little about books and take some of your transactions and show you how to enter them. Is that right?"

"Yes," Ignatz said.

"Okay, I'll give you a general explanation first. . ."

THE FIRST TRANSFORMATION—THE BOOKS

To make sense of all the thousands of transactions that the average business has during the year, these transactions are entered into a daily book called the *journal*. It allows the business to keep track of every daily transaction in one place. Transactions are recorded sequentially, as they happen.

However, if a businessperson wants to find out how much was paid for office supplies in the last two months, he or she would have a problem. Even with the journal, he or she would have to look through *every* transaction in the last two months in order to pick out the supplies purchases in order to obtain a total. To solve this problem a business needed another book that categorized everything under specific topics, or accounts. They needed to have a book that had one page called "office supplies" that listed every office supply expense. This summary book has come to be known as a *ledger*.

Figure 4.1 is an illustration of the transaction sequence from purchase, to original records of the transaction, to "journalizing," to entry in the ledger.

Chart of Accounts

A common practice among most businesses is to assign various accounts a number in addition to a name. For instance, the cash account could have a number '101' so that when making entries the number can be used instead of writing out the name. Using numbers instead of names of accounts is not only easier, but it also lends itself very readily to computerization.

When we give all the accounts numbers, the list of account names and numbers is called a *chart of accounts*.

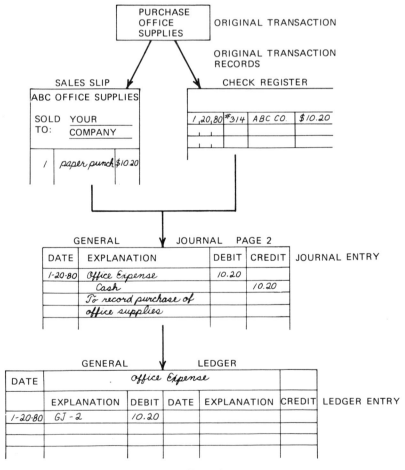

Figure 4.1

The following is a list of assets, liabilities, and expenses that are generally considered to be common account names:

Assets

Cash

Inventory

Accounts receivable (sales that have not been collected)

Notes receivable (short term money owed to your company)

Prepaid expenses (money advanced for services or goods not yet received)

Short-term investments

Equipment (for business use)

Land and buildings (for business use)

Leasehold improvements

Goodwill paid when the business was acquired

Long-term investments

Certain development costs

Liabilities

Accounts and notes payable

Provisions for pensions and taxes

Accrued items

Mortgages

Bonds and debentures

Long-term debt

Deferred taxes

Expenses

Rent or leases (for equipment or real property)

Outside services (accounting, consulting, janitorial, trash pick up, security, etc.)

Personnel salaries

Payroll taxes and benefit plans for employees

Travel required for business purposes

Supplies purchased

Freight

Utilities

Business license and local taxes

Equipment or tools with a life of one year or less

Repairs and maintenance

When we arrange all of these accounts under the basic groups—assets, liabilities, equity, income, and expenses—to simplify identification we have a "chart of accounts".

In developing an index or chart of accounts, blocks of numbers are assigned to each group of accounts. For example, assets are assigned the block of numbers from 100 to 199 (or 1000 to 1999 for large companies with many accounts); liabilities have the numbers 200 to 299 (or 2000 to 2999); and so on.

CHART OF ACCOUNTS

Account number	Account name
100–199	ASSETS
101	Cash
110	Accounts receivable
115	Notes receivable
120	Prepaid expense
120.1	Prepaid rent
150	Equipment
150.18	1970 Dodge pick-up Truck
. . .	Etc.
200–299	LIABILITIES
201	Accounts payable
201.29	Accounts payable— Associated Wagontongues
211	Notes payable
211.2	Notes payable Bank of Suez
221	Taxes payable
. . .	Etc.
300–399	OWNERS' EQUITY
301	Capital stock
310	Preferred stock
330	Retained earnings
. . .	Etc.
400–499	INCOME
401	Income from operations
401.3	Income from Model B solid state mousetrap
401.5	Income from mousetrap accessories
410	Interest income
450	Income from extraordinary items
. . .	Etc.
500–599	OPERATING EXPENSE
501	Salary expense
501.7	Officer's salary
505	Payroll taxes
505.2	Administrative employees payroll tax
508	Rent expense
572	Small tool expense
. . .	Etc.

JOURNALS (THE DAILY BOOKS)

General Journal

The general journal was developed to cover all types of entries. The general journal (Figure 4.2) is a form that has a space for:

1. The date
2. A description of the entry
3. The account number (from the chart of accounts)
4. A check space to check off the entry when it is transferred to the ledger
5. Spaces for debit or credit entries

Every accounting transaction can be recorded in the general journal, and for the very small one-person operation, especially service businesses, this general journal is all that is needed.

"Okay," Pete Popstein stopped and lit his pipe. "Now let's talk about your business here. Let's talk about your books. What I'm going to do is ask you some questions, look at certain documents and make up the entries in your books. Then I'll show you the entries and talk about that they mean. Is that all right?" Pete reached for the adding machine that he had carried in under his arm.

"Yes, that seems like a good way to do it." Lazarus and Ignatz both agreed.

"Okay. Do you have a business checking account?" Pete asked.

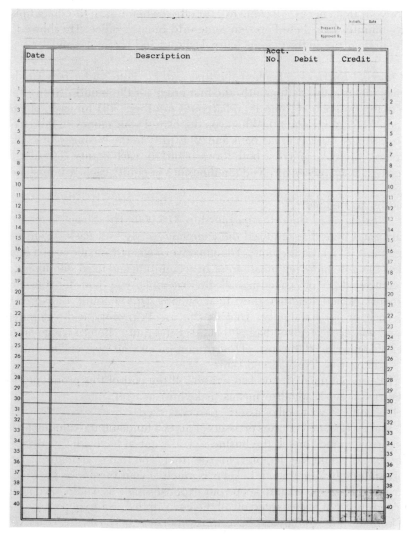

Figure 4.2

"Yes. We opened it before we had any expenses so we could keep track of everything."

"Good, good," Pete said. "This will save us a lot of time. Give me the first month's checks and deposits." Laz handed him a box with checks and deposits in it. "Ah, here. This $20,000—that was your first deposit on June 1. What was it from?"

"Laz and I put in $10,000 in cash each to start the business."

"Good. This next deposit of $15,000. What was that for?"

"Let's see," Laz looked at the deposit slip, "Oh, yeah. Ignatz loaned the company $15,000 to get us started. That was a couple of days after we deposited our ten grand cash each."

"Yes. On the fourth of June," Pete continued. "Now, you guys told me that you put some money into this long before you officially started the partnership. Did you keep the receipts for the equipment you bought? The receipts for all the money you spent developing the prototype are important."

Ignatz got up and walked across the room as he answered. "Yes, I kept all the receipts, and they're in this box." He pulled out a small white box and handed it to Pete.

Pete went through the receipts, got out a pad, and started writing. "This will take a while. Why don't you guys get some coffee?" He said. "I'll do this and make some entries for your first checks. I'll come to your office when I have the sheet finished."

Twenty minutes later Pete Popstein came into Ignatz's office. He showed Laz and Ignatz the first entries in the general journal (shown in Figures 4.3 and 4.4).

General Journal Entries. "Look at the first entry", Pete said. "It is labeled 6-1". That means that it is the sixth month, the first entry for the month. Notice that there is a date of the transaction (June 1) and account numbers (101 for cash, 301 for Time equity and 302 for Whiz equity). When you deposited your money in the account you created two things: (1) cash in the bank and (2) Equity in the business for each owner.

"Therefore, we make an entry both for cash and for each equity. Twenty thousand was deposited. Each owner received ten thousand in equity each. Understand?" Pete paused.

Laz and Ignatz nodded.

"Okay. Next Ignatz loaned the partnership $15,000. The business received cash and Ignatz got a note that required the company to pay him back." Pete held up a legal document. "Here is the note. You guys were smart to make it in a legal form. This makes the note more legitimate from an accounting and legal standpoint."

Pete continued, "You gave me all the receipts you had for the prototype development. Added together they total $6388. This amount I divided equally between each owner for equity. That is, the asset "prototype development" was created and you each received half of that asset in equity. Before we go on, tell me, did either of you write off the costs of this prototype on your personal income tax?"

"No," said Lazarus. "No," agreed Whiz.

"Okay." Pete continued "If you had written off the cost of this prototype, we could not capitalize it now. "Capitalize"means 'make into an asset.'"

"Which is better—write-off or asset?" Lazarus asked.

"Well, that's a question of taxes or assets. This is a fundamental dilemma. If you are going to borrow money or sell the business, you want to have a lot of assets. In that case, the bank would be happier to see that you have capitalized prototype development. On the other hand, to keep as much of your income as possible and not lose it through taxes, you want to keep your expenses high. It would have been better for tax pruposes if you had charged off all the costs of the prototype as expense in this year. Of course, now you almost have to capitalize it because the years you could have written off are gone."

DATE	DESCRIPTION	ACCT.	DEBIT	CREDIT
1981	6-1			
6/1	CASH	101	20000	
	EQUITY - LAZARUS TIME	301		10000
	- IGNATZ WHIZ	302		10000
	TO RECORD CASH CONTRIBUTION OF OWNERS TIME AND WHIZ AS OWNERS' EQUITY			
	6-2			
6/4	CASH	101	15000	
	NOTE PAYABLE - IGNATZ WHIZ	210		15000
	TO RECORD LOAN FROM IGNATZ WHIZ			
	6-3			
6/4	PROTOTYPE DEVELOPMENT	130	6388	
	EQUITY - L. TIME	301		3194
	- I. WHIZ	302		3194
	TO RECORD CAPITALIZATION OF THE COST OF PROTOTYPE DEVELOPMENT. SUMMARIZED FROM ORIGINAL RECEIPTS AND DISTRIBUTED EVENLY BETWEEN TIME AND WHIZ.			

Figure 4.3

Pete continued. "The next two entries—6/4 and 6/5—are for checks you wrote. The first one was for the check you wrote to Rainbow Real Estate. Even though it was only one check, it paid for four items. The first month's rent and the rental commission part of the total cost were expenses. The last month's rent is considered "prepaid rent" and is an asset. When rental deposits are refundable they are assets. That is, you will get the money back in the future. This check for $3650, of course, reduced cash by $3650."

"And lastly you had some shelves and other areas built here at 777 Space Walk Road. These are leasehold improvements. They cost you $3651. You wrote a check for this amount, reducing cash. Do you understand everything so far?" Pete asked.

"Yeah," Lazarus added, "But there is one thing that I'd like to know. How come there are two columns, one marked 'Debit' and one marked 'Credit'? Also, how do you determine what figure goes into what column? I noticed that cash is in one column one time and in another column down the page."

"That's a good question," Pete said. "Debit means left side. Credit means right side. Some accounts—like cash and other assets, expenses, and cost of sales—are

DATE	DESCRIPTION	ACCT.	DEBIT	CREDIT

6-4

DATE	DESCRIPTION	ACCT.	DEBIT	CREDIT
6/6	RENT EXPENSE	508	500	
	PRE-PAID RENT	120	500	
	RENTAL COMMISSION	509	1250	
	RENTAL DEPOSITS	125	1400	
	CASH	101		3650
	TO RECORD PAYMENT OF FIRST AND LAST MONTHS RENT, COMMISSION AND DEPOSITS FOR 777 SPACE WALK RD.			

6-5

DATE	DESCRIPTION	ACCT.	DEBIT	CREDIT
6/10	LEASEHOLD IMPROVEMENTS	140	3651	
	CASH	101		3651
	TO RECORD PAYMENT OF LIMPHAND INTERIORS FOR FIXTURES			

Figure 4.4

increased with a debit. That is, when you deposit cash into your checking account—whether it's from equity, debt, or income from customers—the amount of cash in the account increases. This increase is considered a 'debit' to cash.

"If on the other hand, you paid out something—you wrote a check for rent—cash is decreased. A decrease in cash is shown by a credit.

"This is the double entry bookkeeping system. In the double entry system every entry is made twice—once in a debit column and once in the credit column. Every debit has to equal a corresponding credit and vice versa.

"Debits and credits are confusing to most people, so I've devised a little chart that shows you at a glance which accounts are debited, which are credited, and when." (See Figure 4.5.)

Asset Group	Dollar Amount of Account Increased	Dollar Amount of Account Decreased
Assets	Debit	Credit
Expenses	Debit	Credit
Cost of sales	Debit	Credit
Liabilities	Credit	Debit
Equity	Credit	Debit
Income	Credit	Debit

Figure 4.5

Specialized Journals

"Most businesses use specialized journals to keep track of transactions. These special journals include a *cash disbursements journal* and a *cash receipts journal*. If you sell or buy on credit, you also could have a *sales journal* (if you sell on credit), and a *purchases journal* (if you buy goods on credit).

"I'll explain about each of these in turn, but first I'll go to the office and prepare the books."

Laz and Ignatz agreed to this, and Pete Popstein went off to begin work.

The next afternoon Popstein came back and started to explain. . . .

Cash Disbursements Journal. The cash disbursements journal is a specialized journal designed to record all cash expenditures—usually checks. The cash disbursements journal is comparable to the check register because it records all the checks written. It differs from the check register in that it has special columns for accounts for which many checks are written. For instance, payments of accounts payable and purchases of inventory for cash might require a large number of checks to be written monthly, so the cash disbursements journal has special columns for these items.

The cash disbursements journal allows you to show on one line both the debit (to the account the check is made out to) and the credit (cash) in each transaction. Figure 4.6 is an example of a cash disbursements journal page.

The cash disbursements journal also has a check ($\sqrt{}$) column to show when the accounts were posted to a ledger.

Cash Disbursements Journal Examples. Pete Popstein realized that the business was going to be paying out a lot of checks for expenses, reducing debt, and other purchases in the business, so he started a cash disbursements journal. The entries would be made more easily, and summaries of the transactions would not have to be written every time a check was paid. He figured that he should have special columns for accounts payable since W.T. Technologies required inventory purchases on credit. He included a column for subcontract work.

Example 1. Lazarus writes a check to Titan Telephone for telephone installation and deposits. It is check number 104 and it is written on January 6 for $430, $300 for installation expense and $130 as a deposit.

The original transaction documents include a receipt from Titan Telephone, Inc. and a check from W.T. Technologies. The cash disbursements journal entry is shown in Figure 4.7.

CASH DISBURSEMENTS JOURNAL   FOR MONTH OF _____ 19 ___ PAGE _____

| DATE | CHECK NO. | EXPLANATION | SUNDRY – DEBITS | | | ACCTS. PAY. | | SUB–CONT. | CASH |
			ACCT. NO.	✓	AMOUNT	✓	DR. 201	CR 600–610	IN BANK CR. 101

Figure 4.6

Telephone expense and telephone deposits are debited (increased) and cash is credited (decreased). The transaction involves both an increase (deposits) and a decrease (cash) in assets and an increase in expense.

Example 2. W.T. needs to pay off some of the money that they owe Limphand Interiors. Lazarus writes check 105 for $5000 to Limphand on June 6.

The original transaction document is a check from W.T. Technologies. The cash disbursements journal entry is shown in Figure 4.7.

Accounts payable (account number 201) is debited (decreased) and cash in the bank (account 101) is credited (decreased). The transaction involves a decrease in both a liability (accounts payable) and an asset (cash).

Example 3. W.T. pays Assemblies, Inc., for subcontract work performed—a market analysis. W.T. writes check 106 for $1200.

The transaction documents include a check from W.T. and a paid receipt from Assemblies, Inc. The cash disbursement journal entry is shown in Figure 4.7.

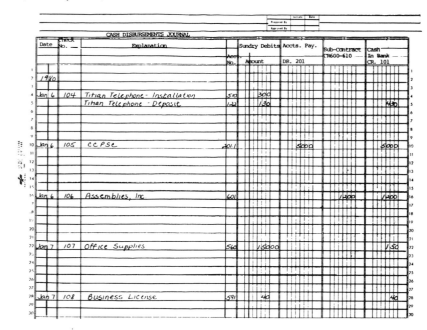

Figure 4.7

Subcontract expense (610) is debited (increased) and cash is credited (decreased). The transaction involves an increase in a cost of sales (subcontract) and a decrease in an asset (cash).

Example 4. W.T. writes check 107 on June 7 to ABC Office Supply for $150.

The transaction documents include a check from W.T. and a sales receipt from ABC Office Supply. The cash disbursements journal entry is Figure 4.7.

Sundry debits—office supplies (560) is debited (increased) and cash is credited (decreased). The transaction involves an increase in expense (office supplies) and a decrease in an asset (cash).

Note. The cash disbursements journal has columnar entries for accounts that will have many transactions (such as cash and accounts payable). Cash is credited in every entry because every time a check is written (a cash disbursement is made), cash is reduced.

The Cash Receipts Journal.   Pete Popstein expected the company to have sales and he found that the first sales he entered would be for cash. Rather than use the general journal he decided to use a cash receipts journal. The cash receipts journal records cash sales and can record sales from different categories in separate columns. For management reasons, Laz wants to keep track of which of his sales are for general consulting and which are for financial consulting. An example of a blank cash disbursements journal is shown in Figure 4.8.

Figure 4.9 shows the cash receipts journal for three months (W.T. Technologies makes only makes a few sales per month).

On June 10, W.T. Technologies sold a holographic memory machine to IBM for $40,000 in cash. This resulted in a debit (increase) in cash of $40,000 and increase (credit) to sales of the same amount.

On June 30 Fairchild paid W.T. $42,000 for a machine that they had bought on credit 15 days earlier. This is represented by a debit (increase) in cash and a credit

DATE		ACCT. NO.	AMOUNT	ACCOUNTS RECEI.	SUPPLIES	CASH IN BANK	CASH SALES

Figure 4.8

		ACC. NO.	CRED. AMT.	ACCOUNTS RECEI. CR. 111	CASH SALES CR. 410	CASH IN BANK DR. 101
1981						
June 10	IBM				40000	40000
Jun 30	Fairchild			42000		42000
July 1	IBM -Supplies	430	1250			1250
July 15	Texas Instruments				40000	40000
Aug 7	Fairchild -repairs	440	1000			1000

Figure 4.9

(decrease) in the asset accounts receivable. When an accounts receivable is paid off, the accounts receivable account is reduced.

On July 1 IBM bought some supplies from W.T. for $1250 in cash. These supplies represented magnetic tape and other gear for the holographic memory machine. The sale of these supplies, even though they are not the main business of W.T., is also considered sales. In the case of supplies, the amount credited (increase in sales) is posted to a special sales account, number 430. Cash is increased (debited) $1250 and supply sales is increased (credited) by $1250.

On July 15 Texas Instruments bought a machine for cash for $40,000. This is shown as a debit to cash (increase) and a credit (increase) to sales.

The last entry is for $1000 in repair services rendered by W.T. for Fairchild. Since this is a special sales category, account number 440, the credit entry is made in the sundry credits column.

Note. The most active column is the sales column in the cash receipts journal. Remember that these are only cash sales and do not include sales made on credit (reserved for the "Sales Journal," discussed next). Cash receipts from whatever source (machine sales, supply sales, and repair services) are entered in the cash receipts journal. Every entry made requires debiting cash.

DATE	SALES SLIP NO.	CUSTOMER'S NAME	✓	ACCOUNTS RECEIVABLE DR. 111	H.M. MACHINE & GENERAL FEES	OTHER SALES & FINANCIAL FEES

Figure 4.10

44

Sales Journal. Because of the quality of their customers, W.T. Technologies decided that the company could extend credit to good customers. This allowed customers to pay for services within a period of thirty (30) days. In order to keep track of his customers, John decided to institute a special journal called the *sales journal*. (A sample sales journal page is shown in Figure 4.10.)

The purpose of the sales journal is to record all accounts receivable as they are created by the customer and record these sales on credit as part of the gross sales of the company.

The sales journal does not record *all* sales, *only* those sales on credit. Figure 4.11 shows W.T. Technology's sales journal.

On June 15, W.T. sold Fairchild a machine for $42,000. This transaction is shown as a debit (increase) to accounts receivable and a credit (increase) in sales of $42,000 each. The sales slip used was number 100. Only July 15 W.T. sold another machine for $42,000 on credit to IBM.

On August 1, W.T. sold Texas Instruments both a $41,000 machine (sales slip 102) and $1000 in supplies. Notice that the accounts receivable column records total accounts receivable of $42,100. In the other sales column $1100 is recorded for supply sales and in the holographic machine sales column, the $41,000 machine price is shown. The August 30 entry is similar except it shows $800 for repairs. Machine sales are $41,500 and total sales to General Motors is $42,300.

DATE	SALES SLIP NO.	CUSTOMER'S NAME	ACCOUNTS RECEIVABLE DR. 111	H.M.MACHINE GENERAL FEES	OTHER SALE FINANCIAL FEES
1980					
6/15	100	FAIRCHILD	42000	42000	
7/15	101	IBM	41000	41000	
8/1	102	TEXAS INSTRUMENTS		41000	
	103	TEXAS INSTRUMENTS-SUPPLIES	42100		1100
8/30	104	GENERAL MOTORS		41500	
	105	GENERAL MOTORS-REPAIRS	42300		800
9/2	106	TRW	41000	41000	

Figure 4.11

The September 2, 1981 sale to TRW is for one machine at $41,000. The transaction is recorded as a $41,000 debit to accounts receivable and a $41,000 credit (increase) to sales.

Note.   The sales journal has a column for the credit slip number or billing document reference which could save a lot of time when tracing down the orders in the future. Accounts receivable is always debited when an entry is made.

Purchases Journal.   Figure 4.12 is a sample purchases journal form. The purchases journal is used to keep track of goods bought from suppliers on credit. This is sometimes called trade credit. The purchases journal is used to record the company's accounts payable as they are incurred. The purchases journal only has entries for the goods purchased on credit, never for cash payments. When you pay off the money you owe to the suppliers, the entry should appear in the cash disbursements journal.

The purchases journal has a column for the date, the name of the supplier, the number of the supplier's invoice, the supplier's terms of payments, and a column for credits to accounts payable and debits to inventory.

Very seldom would a service company like Lazarus's consulting business have a purchases journal. The business that requires a purchases journal most is a manufacturer.

Example 1.   On June 18, W.T. Technologies bought some merchandise from Computer and Circuits Parts Supply Company (CCPSC) for $2000 on credit.

The original transaction document is an invoice (number 10311) dated 1/14/80 from CCPSC. The terms are 2/10 net 30. This means that if W.T. pays for the merchandise in 10 days it will receive a 2% discount from the invoice amount. If W.T. does not take advantage of this document, it has 30 days to pay for the merchandise (see Figure 4.13).

The transaction involves an increase (debit) in the expense inventory purchases and an increase (credit) in the liability accounts payable.

					Accounts Payable	Inventory Purchases
Date	Purchased From	In. No.	In. Date	Terms	CR. 201	DR. 601

Figure 4.12

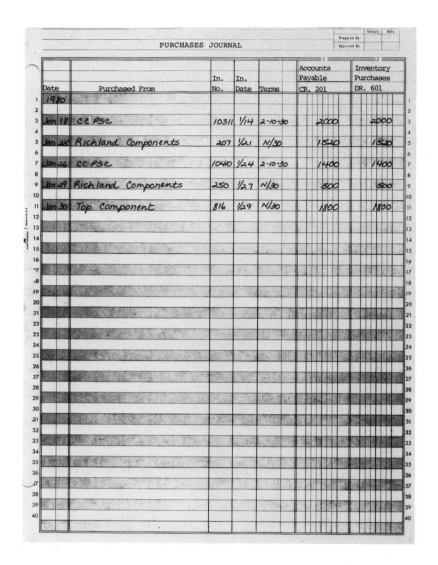

	Date	Purchased From	In. No.	In. Date	Terms	Accounts Payable CR. 201	Inventory Purchases DR. 601	
1	1980							1
2								2
3	Jan 18	CC PSC	10311	1/14	2-10-30	2000	2000	3
4								4
5	Jan 25	Richland Components	207	1/21	N/30	1520	1520	5
6								6
7	Jan 26	CC PSC	10410	1/24	2-10-30	1400	1400	7
8								8
9	Jan 29	Richland Components	250	1/27	N/30	500	500	9
10								10
11	Jan 30	Top Component	816	1/29	N/30	1800	1800	11

PURCHASES JOURNAL

Figure 4.13

Example 2. On June 25 W.T. buys merchandise on credit from Richland Components.

The original transaction document is Richland's invoice (number 207) dated 1/21/80 with net 30 day terms. Richland Components does not offer a discount and their normal terms are payment due in 30 days (see Figure 4.13).

The transaction, as is the case with all other examples in the purchases journal, increases inventory purchases (debit) and increases accounts payable (credit).

Example 3. On June 26, W.T. bought some more merchandise on credit from CCPSC. The original transaction document is the invoice number 10410 from CCPSC (see Figure 4.13).

The transaction involves an increase in both inventory purchase (debit) and accounts payable (credit).

Example 4. On the 29th of June, W.T. bought $500 worth of components on credit from Richland Components. The original transaction document is invoice 250 issued by Richland (see Figure 4.13).

The transaction is increased in the expense inventory purchases (debit) and the liability accounts payable (credit).

Example 5. On June 30, W.T. purchased $1800 worth of merchandise from Top Component, invoice number 816 with net 30 day terms (see Figure 4.13).

The transaction involves an increase (debit) in inventory purchases and an increase in accounts payable (credit).

Note. Every transaction involves a debit to inventory purchases and a credit to accounts payable. Listing the invoice number, date, and terms will help avoid unnecessary problems in the future.

LEDGERS (THE SUMMARY BOOKS)

Now W.T. Technologies has a good handle on all their accounting transactions because they have recorded them chronologically under the special journals. If they want to review the checks they have written in a given period, they look at the cash disbursements journal. They can track their purchases, cash receipts, credit sales, and other transactions in total—and in chronological order—without viewing the original checks.

But what if W.T. wants to find out what IBM bought from them during the last year, or how much they spent on utilities?

One way to find these totals is to go back through the journals during the entire period, locate the separate items, and then total them. Another way would be to write or call the supplier, customer, or utility company and ask them how much you owe. The best way, however, is to keep a summary book, during the period, transferring each entry to a particular category. In other words, if you could have a book that listed each account separately (a page for utilities, a page for rent, etc.) you could tell at a glance how much you owe, who owes you, or how much you've already paid.

A book that lists each account under a separate category is called a *ledger*. Weekly, monthly, or quarterly, all the journals are totaled and "posted" into ledgers. Ledgers are summaries of activities under each account in the chart of accounts. Ledgers are divided into two groups: the general ledger and the subsidiary ledgers.

Historically, there was only the *general ledger*. In the general ledger, all the accounts were posted after a given period from their respective journals. Entries in the journal indicate to the accountant what is to be debited and what is to be credited. With the journals as a guide, the information is entered into the respective individual accounts. The accountant uses printed forms for his account records, as illustrated in Figure 4.14. Each account is kept on a separate form called a ledger sheet. All the accounts taken together constitute a ledger or "book of final entry." Some accountants make up a balance sheet and profit and loss statement and post from these statements into the ledger. But generally the ledger is posted from the journals. Eventually a "trial balance" is made and this is put into the form of a balance sheet and income statement (profit and loss statement). The ledger is the master reference book of the accounting system and provides a permanent and classified record of every element involved in the business operation.

The general ledger is divided into separate accounts (e.g., "cash 101") with a debit and credit column for each account. A look at the ledger account record will reveal a complete history of the increases and decreases of the items involved. Ledgers may

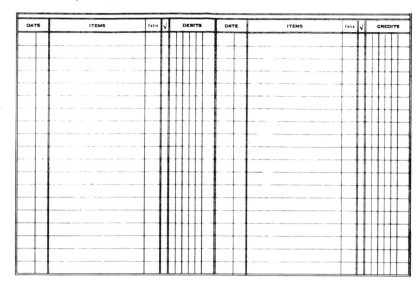

DATE	ITEMS	Folio	√	DEBITS	DATE	ITEMS	Folio	√	CREDITS

Figure 4.14

be kept in book or card form in a ledger tray. Or, of course, these records may be kept on a computer.

General Ledger Format

Figure 4.14 shows a general ledger format. Note that the format has a column for the date. The date used here may either be the date the entry was made in a journal or the date that the entry was transferred from the journal to the ledger. The former is preferable, but either is acceptable as long as the system is consistent.

There are two columns for explanation and two for posting reference. This allows an explanation and a posting reference for a debit and credit entry separately. The explanation is usually something like "total 1/15/78" or the name the check was made payable to, such as "Titan Telephone" for the telephone deposit entry.

The *posting reference* refers to the journal that is the source of the entry. Generally in the post reference, the type of journal and the page number is given. However, in the general journal, a journal entry number is used. For instance, if a total for cash disbursed (credit to cash) is taken from the cash disbursement journal at the end of the month, the post reference would be "CDJ-1," which means the entry comes from the cash disbursement journal, page 1. General journal summaries would have post references like "CJ-1-5" meaning general journal, entry 1-5—the fifth entry (5) for the month of January (1).

The abbreviations that are commonly used for the post reference are shown in Figure 4.15.

Name of Journal	Abbreviations Used
General journal	GJ
Cash disbursements journal	CDJ
Cash receipts journal	CRJ
Sales journal	SJ

Figure 4.15 Table of journal abbreviations.

The ledger format is divided into a debit and a credit side. If the entry is a credit, it is entered on the credit side; if a debit it is entered on the debit side.

Note also that the format has a line at the top and a space for the number of the account. The line should be filled in with the name of the account and the number space should be filled in with the number of the account from the chart of accounts. The accounts are usually in the general journal in order of their chart of account numbers. The first account entered is usually "cash," "Cash in Bank," or "Cash in Bank (Amerigold)," plus the account number such as "101."

The journal entries used in the first part of this chapter for W.T. Technologies (Figures 4.3 through 4.13) will now be posted to the proper general ledger and special ledger accounts. First the completed general ledger is shown in Figure 4.16. A discussion of each account follows.

CASH   #101

DATE	ITEMS	Folio	√	DEBITS	DATE	ITEMS	Folio	√	CREDITS
1981					1981				
6/1	GJ 6-1			20000	6/6	GJ 6-4			3650
6/4	GJ 6-2			15000	6/10	GJ 6-5			3651
8/7	CRJ-1			124250	6/7	CDJ-1			6820

ACCOUNTS RECEIVABLE   #111

DATE	ITEMS	Folio	√	DEBITS	DATE	ITEMS	Folio	√	CREDITS
1981					1981				
9/2	SJ-1			208400	8/7	CRJ-1			42000

PREPAID RENT   #120

DATE	ITEMS	Folio	√	DEBITS	DATE	ITEMS	Folio	√	CREDITS
1981									
6/6	GJ 6-4			500					

Figure 4.16

TELEPHONE DEPOSITS #122

DATE	ITEMS	folio	√	DEBITS	DATE	ITEMS	folio	√	CREDITS
1981									
6/6	CDJ-1			130					

RENTAL DEPOSITS #125

DATE	ITEMS	folio	√	DEBITS	DATE	ITEMS	folio	√	CREDITS
1981									
6/6	GJ 6-4			1400					

PROTOTYPE DEVELOPMENT #130

DATE	ITEMS	folio	√	DEBITS	DATE	ITEMS	folio	√	CREDITS
1981									
6/4	GJ 6-4			6388					

LEASEHOLD IMPROVEMENTS #140

DATE	ITEMS	folio	√	DEBITS	DATE	ITEMS	folio	√	CREDITS
1981									
6/10	GJ 6-5			3651					

ACCOUNTS PAYABLE #201

DATE	ITEMS	folio	√	DEBITS	DATE	ITEMS	folio	√	CREDITS
1981					1981				
6/6	CDJ-1			5000	6/30	PJ-1			7220

Figure 4.16 *(Continued)*

NOTES PAYABLE - I. C. WHIZ   #210

DATE	ITEMS	Folio	√	DEBITS	DATE	ITEMS	Folio	√	CREDITS
					_1981_				
					6/4	GJ 6-2			15000

EQUITY - LAZARUS TIME   #301

DATE	ITEMS	Folio	√	DEBITS	DATE	ITEMS	Folio	√	CREDITS
					_1981_				
					6/1	GJ 6-1			10000
					6/4	GJ 6-3			3194

EQUITY - IGNATZ CULVER WHIZ   #302

DATE	ITEMS	Folio	√	DEBITS	DATE	ITEMS	Folio	√	CREDITS
					_1981_				
					6/1	GJ 6-1			10000
					6/4	GJ 6-3			3194

HOLOGRAPHIC MEMORY SALES   #440

DATE	ITEMS	Folio	√	DEBITS	DATE	ITEMS	Folio	√	CREDITS
					_1981_				
					8/7	CRJ-1			80000
					9/2	SJ-1			206500

Figure 4.16   *(Continued)*

SUPPLY SALES #430

DATE	ITEMS	folio	√	DEBITS	DATE	ITEMS	folio	√	CREDITS
					1981				
					7/1	CRJ-1			1250
					8/1	SJ-1			1100

REPAIR SERVICES #440

DATE	ITEMS	folio	√	DEBITS	DATE	ITEMS	folio	√	CREDITS
					1981				
					8/7	CRJ-1			1000
					8/30	SJ-1			800

RENTAL EXPENSE #508

DATE	ITEMS	folio	√	DEBITS	DATE	ITEMS	folio	√	CREDITS
1981									
6/6	GJ 6-4			500					

RENTAL COMMISSION #509

DATE	ITEMS	folio	√	DEBITS	DATE	ITEMS	folio	√	CREDITS
1981									
6/6	GJ 6-4			1250					

Figure 4.16 *(Continued)*

TELEPHONE   #510

DATE	ITEMS	Folio	√	DEBITS	DATE	ITEMS	Folio	√	CREDITS
1981									
6/6	CDJ-1			300					

OFFICE SUPPLIES   #560

DATE	ITEMS	Folio	√	DEBITS	DATE	ITEMS	Folio	√	CREDITS
1981									
6/7	CDJ-1			150					

BUSINESS   LICENSE   #591

DATE	ITEMS	Folio	√	DEBITS	DATE	ITEMS	Folio	√	CREDITS
1981									
6/6	.CDJ-1			40					

INVENTORY   PURCHASES   #601

DATE	ITEMS	Folio	√	DEBITS	DATE	ITEMS	Folio	√	CREDITS
1981									
6/30	PJ-1			7220					

Figure 4.16   *(Continued)*

General Comments.   All entries from the general journal are posted to the Ledger. Special journals—the cash disbursements, cash receipts, and sales journals—are different. In the special journals, the columns that have the most activities are *added* up at the end of a period and their *totals* are posted to the ledger. Figure 4.17 shows each journal and the columns from each journal that are totaled at the end of the period.

Journal	Account Columns Totaled and Posted
General journal	None
Cash disbursements journals	Cash in bank
	Accounts payable
	All other columns except sundry debits
Cash receipts journal	Cash in bank
	Accounts receivable
	Income accounts except sundry credits
Sales journal	Accounts receivable
	All income accounts

Figure 4.17   Account columns totaled.

In the special journals, the columns that are not totalled are the "sundry" columns, either "sundry debits" or "sundry credits." In the general journal, no totals are obtained and each entry is posted in the ledger separately.

The traditional technique of totaling a column in a special journal is called footing. Footing is simply the process of drawing a line at the bottom of the column in pencil and writing the total under the line in pencil.

The cash account (number 101) in the general ledger example has the most entries from the journals (six) which is a typical situation. The first two entries on the debit side and the first two entries on the credit side came from the general ledger (GJ in the post reference column). All entries from the general journal are posted to the ledger. The last (third) entry on the debit side is the cash debit total from June 1 through August 7, from the cash receipts journal (CRJ). The last (third) entry on the credit side is the cash credit total from the cash disbursements journal from June 1 through June 7.

The accounts receivable account (number 111) has only one entry. This is a debit entry of $2084 which is the column total from the sales journal (SJ), page 1. Each separate customer account transaction is usually posted in a special ledger known as the accounts receivable ledger. Only the total of the accounts receivable—*customer credit extended*—and the payments made on these accounts are entered in the accounts receivable ledger account in the general journal. This account is sometimes called the "accounts receivable control account."

The prepaid rent account (number 120) has one entry which is for the last month's rent recorded in the General Journal (GJ) on June 6.

Telephone Deposits (number 122) is an asset account with one entry. The entry is from the cash disbursements journal. *Rental deposits* also has one entry, this one from the general journal (entry 6-4 from June 6). Since deposits are an asset that generally represent money that will not become an expense until some time in the future, most entries are debit (increasing) entries.

Prototype development (number 130) is the value of the asset prototype. There is one entry from the general journal (6-4). This account will only be decreased (credited) when amoritization is applied to the asset. Generally it will have a debit balance.

The *Leasehold improvements account* (number 110) has one entry which represents the initial leasehold improvements purchase, which is an asset. The entry comes from the general journal, entry 6-5 (GJ 6-5).

Note on all 100 accounts.   All accounts from 100 to 199 are asset accounts. This means that generally they will have a debit balance, and the majority of the entries will be debit entries. Cash and accounts receivable are the only accounts that will receive frequent credit entries.

The accounts payable account (number 201) has two entries. The only debit entry is the total of all accounts payable paid in cash for that period from the cash disbursements journal, page 1 (CDJ-1). The entry (June 30) on the credit side of the accounts payable ledger is from the purchases journal (PJ-1).

Notes Payable—Ignatz Whiz (number 210) has one credit entry. This entry records the total amount of the loan from the general journal (GJ 6-2). Each time the company secures a loan it will be a credit entry for the total amount. This account will have debit entries each time the principal portion of the loan is paid. Each month or quarter that a payment on the loan is made, the interest portion of that payment will be interest expense, and the principal portion of the payment will be a debit to this account.

Note on 200 accounts.   All accounts from 200 to 299 are liability accounts. They generally have *credit* balances. Accounts payable and notes payable accounts will, however, have frequent debit entries. The majority of the loan payable account entries will be debit entries for principal portion payment of debt.

W.T. Technologies is a partnership, therefore there are two equity accounts: one for Lazarus Time and one for Ignatz Culver Whiz. Since each partner is a 50–50 owner and equal contributer to equity, the amounts in the equity accounts are equal.

Equity: Lazarus Time (account number 301) and *Equity: I.C. Whiz* (account 302) both have two credit entries. One is from the general journal, entry 6-1, which is the original $10,000 each that they put into the business. The other entry is from the general journal, entry 6-3, which is half the amount of which the prototype was capitalized.

Note on 300 accounts.   All accounts from 300 to 399 are equity accounts. They generally have credit balances.

Holographic memory sales (number 410) has two entries, both credit entries. One entry is for the sales receipts until August 7 paid for in cash. That entry is from the cash receipts journal, (CRJ-1) page 1. The second credit entry is from the sales journal, page 1 (SJ-1). This represents all the sales on credit until September 2.

Supply sales (number 430) also has an entry from the cash receipts journal (CRJ-1) and the sales journal (SJ-1). The July entry from the cash receipts journal is for cash received for supplies. The entry from the sales journal is for credit sales.

Repair services (number 440) has two credit entries. One entry is from the cash receipts journal (CRJ-1) which represents cash sales. The other credit entry is from the sales journal which represents credit sales.

Note on 400 accounts.   All accounts from 400 to 499 are income accounts. Income accounts always have a credit balance and very, very rarely receive a debit entry. The only debit entry posted in these accounts would be for sales returns and allowances.

Rental expense account (number 508) has a single debit entry, that from the general journal (GJ 6-4).

Rental commission (number 509) has one entry from the general journal (GJ 6-4).

Telephone expense (number 510) has a debit entry from the cash disbursements journal (CDJ-1) for a monthly telephone expense.

Office supplies (number 560) has a debit entry from the cash disbursements journal dated June 7.

Business license expense (number 591) has a debit entry for $40 from the cash disbursements journal.

Note on 500 accounts. All accounts from 500 to 599 are expense accounts. They will always have a debit balance and will, except in rare circumstances, have only debit entries.

Inventory purchases (account 601) has a debit entry from the purchases journal (PJ-1) from June 30.

Notes on 600 accounts. All accounts from 600 to 699 will have debit balances. Almost all of the entries in these accounts will be debit entries. The 600 accounts are the cost of sales accounts and the only credit entries will be for returns of merchandise or discounts.

Special Ledgers (Accounts Receivable and Accounts Payable Ledgers)

It is important for a company to keep careful track of who owes them what. You also want to know how much your customer owes you and for how long: when you billed and how much. The total in the sales journal will tell you the total sales on credit you have, and if you trace through it and separate out the customers, you can find the individual statistics. Most people, however, find that it is much smarter to keep an account for each customer apart from the sales journal. The ledger that keeps track of what each customer is billed and later pays for under the customer's name is called the *accounts receivable ledger*.

Figures 4.18 and 4.19 are samples of the special ledger format. The same format is used for both the accounts receivable ledger and the accounts payable ledger.

The format has a place for the name of the account. This would be the customer's name in the accounts receivable ledger. It also includes a space for the terms such as

Special Ledger Sheet

Account:			No.				
Date	Description	PR	Items posted		Balance		
			Debit	Credit	Debit	Credit	

Figure 4.18

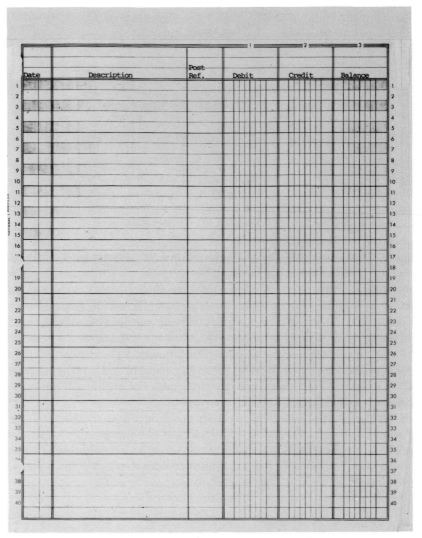

Figure 4.19

net 30 days, 2/10 net 30, and so on. It has a column for the date of the transaction—the date the order was shipped (from the sales journal) or the date the payment was recorded in the cash receipts journal.

It also has a column for a description, which is used for pertinent information such as the invoice number. The post reference column could be used for the name and page number of the special journals or the entry number for the general journal. This is the same column that was used before in the general ledger.

The debit column in the accounts receivable ledger would be for all credit sales to customers recorded in the sales journal. The credit column in the accounts receivable ledger would be used to record payments from the cash receipts journal.

Examples of Special Ledgers.   The following examples are from W.T. Technologies (see Figures 4.3 through 4.13). The special ledgers are posted directly from the journals. The accounts receivables ledger (Figure 4.20) shows five customers: Fairchild, IBM, Texas Instruments, General Motors, and TRW. W.T. Technologies extends 30 day terms.

DATE	DESCRIPTION	POST REF.	DEBIT	CREDIT	BALANCE
	FAIR CHILD	N 30 terms			
1981 Jun 15	SJ-1		42000 -		42000 -
Jun 30	CRJ-1			42000 -	— 0 —
	IBM	N 30 terms			
1981 July 15	SJ-1		41000-		41000 -
	TEXAS INSTRUMENTS	N 30 terms			
1981 aug 1	SJ-1		42100 -		42100 -
	General Motors	N 30 terms			
1981 Aug 30	SJ-1		42300 -		42300 -
	TRW	N 30 terms			
1981 Sept 2	SJ-1		41000 -		41000 -

Figure 4.20

Fairchild was billed $42,000 for merchandise delivered on June 15 as recorded in the sales journal (SJ-1). Fifteen days later Fairchild paid off the $42,000 that they owed W.T. Technologies. Since the payment was in cash, this was recorded in the cash receipts journal (CRJ-1). Notice that the original balance (credit balance) is $42,000. When the amount owed (the accounts receivable for $42,000) is paid off, the balance column is reduced to zero.

The credit entries for IBM, Texas Instruments, General Motors, and TRW are all from the sales journal page one (SJ-1). Since none of these companies have paid for the merchandise, the balance owed column is equal to the original amount of the purchase.

Note on Accounts Receivable Ledger. The accounts receivable ledger generally has a *debit* balance because it is an asset account. All debit entries will come either from the sales journal or the general journal. Credit entries are made when the receivables are paid by the customers. Credit entries will always originate from the cash receipts journal or the general journal.

SUMMARY OF THE FIRST TRANSFORMATION

When a businessperson has the correct books, journals, and ledgers, all financial information required by the IRS, a financial lender, or is available to him or her in an organized format.

The difficulty with journals and ledgers has always been inaccurate entries through human error. Therefore one of the most important rules when making bookkeeping entries is to double check—always. There are several techniques for double checking. The one used most often is the trial balance, which is discussed in the next chapter.

Pete Popstein leaned back and lit his pipe. He pointed to all the schedules on the table. "Well," he said, "now you get the idea. You can see that some of the journals are for the month of June—your first month—and some of them go all the way to August. I wanted to do five examples in each journal so you could use them as an example. Laz told me that you haven't sold much since August, so the first three months sales really distort the picture. Are there any questions?"

Both Laz and Ignatz shook their heads no.

"Okay, you guys can complete these journals and then I'll look at them and make up the financial statements that the bank wants for a loan. Remember, the faster you get me these books, the faster I can do the statements and the faster you get a loan."

After he left, Laz and Ignatz agreed to work on the books in four hour shifts after regular work hours.

Chapter Five

Assets

Pete Popstein had told Lazarus Time that the most important thing to a bank or to a buyer was the assets of the company.

Lazarus now had a good feeling on how to keep track of his business expenses, sales, and resources. But one of the things that he wasn't too familiar with was assets.

Assets include such important items as cash, accounts receivable, and equipment and fixtures such as automobile and leasehold improvements.

One thing that he heard about was "income tax credits." A CPA told him that an income tax credit allowed him to deduct directly off taxes due 10% of the leasehold improvement cost. Plus, he could also write the leasehold improvement and furniture off through depreciation over a longer period. This was hard for Laz to believe. But it was true.

Lazarus was also developing a healthy respect for cash. It was hard to run the business without it. He learned quite quickly that the sales he received were not cash because the sales did not become cash until they were collected. It was a simple matter to bill the client, and something else altogether to collect the bill. So he wanted to find out about how cash and accounts receivable are handled.

So Lazarus was very interested in the class instruction for the evening at university extension. The instructor was going to talk about assets.

When Laz arrived the instructor was talking to one of the students who owned a food importing business. At precisely 6:30 the class began.

"Tonight we are going to talk about assets. Assets are defined as by the IRS as 'property that is used in your business or trade.' These properties—assets— contribute either directly or indirectly towards earning business income.

"First I want to bring up something that Sam Chin just told me about his business. Sam, tell everybody what your philosophy about receivables is."

"My philosophy," Mr. Chin smiled, "is simply this. I carry my receivables in my pocket. I usually don't extend credit to anyone. They pay cash for the goods. But there are a few customers that I have known for three years—most of that time I've known them personally. With them, I allow credit. But they give me a post-dated check. It is dated for 15 days later. Like I said," Chin hit his back pocket, "I carry my receivables in my pocket." Chin pulled out three checks. "I carry it in my wallet until I'm ready to cash it."

Suzi Wo, one of the Chinese ladies in the class, said. "This is the old way of extending credit. For years we have been doing this that way." She giggled, "I guess you could call it 'Chinese receivables.'"

The instructor tried to take control of the class again. "Okay," he said, "Accounts receivables are a very important asset. They are sales that you haven't collected cash for. And everyone knows that 'cash' is the only four-letter word to remember in business."

"All right," the instructor waved his hands. He was in a rare mood tonight. "Let's get serious."

"Assets are productive items which contribute to income. Generally speaking, assets are tangible property like equipment or promises of future receipt of cash, like accounts receivable. . ."

Assets include the following items (accounts):

- Cash
- Accounts receivable
- Inventory
- Investments
- Prepaid expense (such as last month's rent or utility deposits)
- Equipment
- Motor vehicles
- Furniture and fixtures
- Land and buildings
- Building improvements (called leasehold improvements if you are a renter)
- Other tangible property
- Goodwill
- Patents and copyrights
- Organizational expense

All these items can be divided into three categories: current, fixed, and other assets.

Current assets are those items that can be readily converted into cash within a one year period. Current assets are assets in which the flow of funds is one of continuous circulation or turnover in the short run. For service businesses, like business consulting companies, current assets represent the longest group of assets.

Fixed assets are items of property, plant, and equipment and are referred to as "fixed" because of their permanent nature and because they are not subject to rapid turnover. Fixed assets are used in connection with producing or earning revenue and are not for sale in the ordinary course of business.

Other assets are all the assets that are not current and cannot fit into the fixed asset category (such as research and development, or goodwill).

CURRENT ASSETS

Current assets include cash, accounts receivable, inventory, investments (short-term), and prepaid expenses. The more important current assets are cash, accounts receivable, and inventory. Cash and accounts receivable will be discussed in turn.

Cash

The cash account is the most active of all business accounts. Receipts from sales (either in cash or payment of accounts receivable), receipts from the sale of assets, receipts from capital investment of the owners, and receipts of loan proceeds all go through the cash account. Disbursement for payment of expenses, repayment of a liability, payment of dividends or owner's draw, and the purchase of assets all go through the cash account. The cash account is the only account that is used in transactions with all the other groups of accounts: assets, liabilities, capital, income, and expenses.

Cash transactions in the cash account can be roughly divided into (1) cash receipts and payments, and (2) cash documentation in original vouchers, journals, and ledgers. Cash receipts are cash received by the company either as a result of sales of products or assets, or investment in the business, or proceeds from borrowing. Cash documentation involves the bookkeeping system of the company from the original transaction document (such as a sales receipt) to the journals (cash receipts journal) to the ledgers.

Cash Receipts and Payments.   The principal cash events and their related original transaction documents shown in Figure 5.1.

These original transaction documents initiate the processing of cash data. A cash receipt document indicates that the firm has received cash; a check indicates that payment has been made; an adjustment advice informs the bookkeeper to record bank charges in an effort to reconcile a cash account with its related bank statement and so on.

The concept of cash receipt, relocation, and disbursement can be further illustrated in terms of how it affects journal entries as follows (see Figure 5.2).

The following is a list of typical origins of cash receipts and disbursements.

Receipts

1. From customers—collections of accounts receivable or notes payable.
2. From cash sales.
3. From miscellaneous repetitive sources—rent income, interest income, dividends, royalties, sale or surplus assets or investments, and new sources of finance (bank borrowings, loans, equity investment from outside).

Payments

1. To suppliers of raw materials or other supplies—reduction of accounts payable or notes payable.
2. To employees for salaries and labor related expenses—taxes, insurance, pension, etc.

Event	Original Transaction Document (See Chapter 1 for Examples)
Cash is received	Receipt (sales receipt, check cash) Draft (bank deposit slip)
Cash is relocated or transferred	Record of deposit (relocation of cash to a bank account) Transfer (relocation of cash from one business or division to another, or from one bank account to another)
Cash is disbursed	Bank adjustment (reduction from bank account for bank service charges and adjustments) Petty cash fund Check or money order

Figure 5.1   Original transaction documents.

3. Utilities and other services where payment is made on a regular bases—telephone, accounting, maintenance, etc.

4. Other operating expenses—supplies, small tools, fees, etc.

5. Settlement of tax liabilities—federal, state, and local.

6. For capital expenditures—the acquisition of land, buildings, plant, and equipment (representing significant but irregular payments).

7. To meet financial obligations:

 a. Of a regular nature—interest and dividend payments.

 b. Of an irregular nature—repayment of loans.

8. For any other purpose of a significant, irregular, or extraordinary nature—such as settlement of litigation.

Event/Voucher	Notation	Accounts	Debit $	Credit $
Cash is received	Cash provided as equity	Cash	5,000	
Receipt voucher	from owners	Equity		5,000
	Cash provided by	Cash	2,500	
	long-term creditors	Long-term liability		2,500
	Customer pays cash	Cash	150	
	on account	Accounts receivable		150
	Fixed assets sold	Cash	1,000	
	for cash	Fixed asset		1,000
	A sale is made	Cash	1,500	
	for cash	Income		1,500
Cash is relocated				
Deposit	Cash is deposited	X Bank	9,750	
	X Bank	Cash		9,750
	Cash is transferred from	Y Bank	5,000	
	X Bank to Y Bank	X Bank		5,000
Cash is disbursed				
Adjustment	X Bank service charges	Bank charges	5	
	are recorded	X Bank		5
Petty cash	Postage stamps	Miscellaneous expense	50	
	are purchased	Cash		50
Checks	Merchandise is	Inventory	900	
	purchased with a check	X Bank		900
	from X Bank			
	A payment is made to	Long-term liability	500	
	long-term creditors from	X Bank		500
	X Bank			
	Owner takes draw	Owners draw (equity)	1,000	
	from Y Bank	Y Bank		1,000
	Payment is made to	Accounts payable	250	
	vendor from Y Bank	Y Bank		250
	A fixed asset is purchased	Fixed asset	2,500	
	with a check/Y Bank	Y Bank		2,500
	Wages, rent, and	Expenses	400	
	expenses/Y Bank	Y Bank		400
Total			30,505	30,505

Figure 5.2 Cash actions and journal entries.

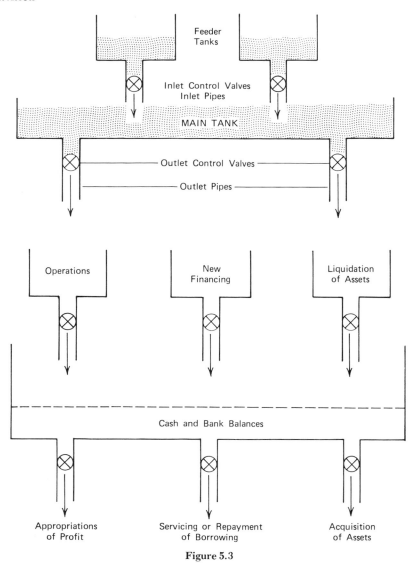

Figure 5.3

The Cash Tank Method of Cash Management. W.C.R. Hartley, in his book *Cash: Planning, Forecasting, and Control.* * describes an easy-to-visualize method of cash management called the *cash tank*.

The level of liquid (cash) in the tank can only be controlled by one of two courses of action: (1) reducing or eliminating outflows by adjusting the valves on one or more of the outlet pipes, or (2) increasing inflows by adjusting the valves on one or more of the inlet pipes.

A schematic diagram of such a liquid flow system appears at the top of Figure 5.3. It shows the main tank, feeder tanks, inlet pipes and outlet pipes with the control valves pictured as a spoked wheel. The control valves regulate both the rate and timing of the flow.

Against the background of this physical model of liquid flow it is easy to visualize a cash flow system that adopts the same concepts. The main elements of such a system are incorporated into the second schematic diagram shown in the Figure 5.3. Only

*London, Business Books, 1976.

three feeder tanks have been used, representing the three major sources: income from operations, new financing (from debt or capital injection), and liquidation of assets.

Similarly, each group of inflows has its counterpart group of outflows: appropriations of profit (payment of all expenses out of income, payment of taxes, owners' draw, dividends, etc.); servicing or repayment of borrowings; and acquisition of assets. If management is to control the level of cash in the tank, these are the three primary groups of inflow and outflow to be addressed.

Forecasting Cash Movements.   Because cash flow is critical to a firm, it is essential that management attempt to forecast the likely pattern of future cash flows, if only as a precaution against business failure. Such a forecast will not always be precisely accurate—nevertheless, it will still create reliable signals to indicate whether, when, and what type of action needs to be taken. A "good" forecast is not necessarily the one that turns out to be "right," but the one that—as the future unfolds—provides the basis for guiding appropriate and timely management action.

There are two types of forecasts: short-term and long-term. Because the two types have slightly different objectives and orientation they will be dealt with separately.

The Short-Term Cash Forecast.   The short-term (or short-range) cash budget covers the length of a cycle from investment of cash to its recovery in such terms as inventory and receivables. The period covered is generally one year.

The prime objective of a short-term cash forecast is to ensure that a firm can pay its debts in the immediate future. It is oriented towards the guidance of appropriate management control action in the short term. For this reason, it needs to be up to date and reasonably detailed. It should be prepared at frequent intervals over the next six to twelve months.

Long-Term Cash Forecast.   A long-term (or long-range) cash forecast covers the length of a cycle from investment of cash to its recovery from such items as plant and equipment, market development, and research. The period most commonly used for this purpose is three to five years, because this is considered the maximum length of time in which sales trends, technology, and the products of market development and research can be projected with sufficient certainty to yield a reliable cash forecast. In cases where long-term cash flow is certain, as with ground rents, mortgage loans or long-term leases, cash flow may be projected accurately for longer periods.

The object of preparing a cash forecast over the longer term is to indicate the financial consequences of future strategic courses of action and to assist in long-term financial planning. This objective is quite different from that of short-term forecasts. The long-term forecast is usually prepared annually. Its orientation is toward the financial consequences of and interrelationships between strategic management decisions.

Cash Control.   There are generally considered to be two types of control in the cash system: (1) stewardship controls and (2) management controls.

Stewardship Controls.   Stewardship controls are designed to accomplish two things: (1) the proper receipt of all cash to the organization and (2) the proper disbursement of all cash by the organization.

Cash is more susceptible to theft than any other asset, and a large percentage of business transactions involve the receipt and disbursement of cash. For these reasons, strict stewardship controls are needed to prevent misappropriation of cash. Two forms of embezzlement should be noted:

1. *Lapping:* The theft of cash received from one customer, but credited to that customer's account at a later day by using cash received from another customer.
2. *Kiting:*
   a. Cashing an unrecorded check in one bank, and covering it with a check drawn on another bank.
   b. Opening a bank account with a fraudulent check (usually originating in a different city or state to lengthen clearing time), and then drawing most of the amount out before the bank discovers the error.

Embezzlement using the methods above, as well as other techniques, may be guarded against by maintaining a system of internal controls over the handling of cash. The following are general principles for controlling cash receipts and cash disbursements.

Controlling cash receipts

1. The immediate separation of cash from its documentation. For instance, people who record cash transactions should not write checks or make deposits. Documentation is channeled to the accounting department and cash to the cashier. Their records can be compared.
2. The function of cash handling must be distinct from maintaining the accounting records. Neither party should have access to or supervise the recordkeeping of the other.
3. If possible, there should be a daily deposit of all cash receipts into the bank.
4. The person responsible for cash receipts should not be responsible for cash disbursements.

Controlling cash disbursements

1. All disbursements should be made by check. Issuing a check should require approval of more than one person. A cancelled check is proof that payment was made, and payment by check provides a permanent record of disbursements.
2. Checks should be prenumbered. Spoiled checks should be marked "void."
3. If possible, checks should be signed by one person and countersigned by another.
4. Supporting invoices and other documentation should be perforated or marked "paid," in order to prevent double payment for the same item.
5. A system for approving payments should underlie the issuance of checks. The person who approved payment should not be the person who issues the check.

Note. stewardship controls place a repeated emphasis on the principle of *separation of duties.* Underlying this principle is the fact that the probabilities of embezzlement decrease significantly where an act of dishonesty requires the collusion of two or more persons.

Management Controls. Management control has as its principal purpose *optimizing* the company's cash position. This is true if the company has a cash surplus or a cash deficit.

Excess cash may denote poor management, as these cash resources can usually producer a higher return if they are converted to some other form of asset (such as investments). Contrary to popular thinking, a large cash balance is not a reliable indicator of an organization's good state of health; it may be just the opposite. Too little cash is also hazardous and may require unscheduled borrowing of funds on adverse terms, or the untimely disposition of the firm's assets.

How does one optimize cash position? The application of management controls in administering cash has had some impressive results.

Cash forecasts and budgets are the principal techniques for the management control of cash. Cash budgets may be prepared for any period of time. They serve as management controls for the following reasons:

1. They emphasize the timing of future cash events.
2. They indicate periods when cash surpluses or shortages are likely to occur, thus enabling management to:
    a. Convert temporary surplus cash into investments.
    b. Arrange in advance for financing for periods where shortages are indicated.
3. They facilitate the scheduling of loan repayments.
4. By distinguishing postponable from nonpostponable disbursements, they provide management with a basis for deciding priorities and for relating postponable needs to periods where optimum financing is possible.
5. They provide guidelines for controlling disbursements, in that expenditures for a particular account cannot exceed budget without special approval.

Financial cash flow ratios are another technique for optimizing management controls of cash.

One ratio for doing this is the *average daily disbursements ratio*. This is a simple ratio that tells you how much your company spends each day on the average. The formula can be represented as follows:

$$AD = \frac{TD}{N}$$

where: AD = average daily disbursements
TD = total disbursements for a period
N = number of days in the period

Once you know the average amount of money the firm spends daily (the average daily disbursements above), then it is easy to find out how long your cash reserve will last if there is no income. You multiply the average daily disbursements by the number of days to be covered by the cash reserve, as follows:

$$C = R \times AD$$

where: C = cash balance
R = number of days covered by the cash reserve
D_a = average daily disbursements (from the previous formula)

If you want to find out how many days the cash reserve will last, just turn the formula around like this:

$$R = \frac{C}{AD}$$

Example: W. T. Technologies wishes to maintain a cash balance equal to 20 days of average daily disbursements. Total disbursements for the year is scheduled to be $360,000. The calculations will be based on a standard financial year of 360 days.

$$AD: \frac{\$360,000}{360} = \$1000$$

$$C: 20 \times \$1000 = \$20,000$$

There are other ratios that assist management in controlling cash flow—in particular, break-even and cash break-even formulas and accounts receivable and inventory ratios. These ratios will be discussed later.

Money *float* is also a very effective management cash control technique. "Float" is cash in transit. For example, the period between the time a check is written and the time it clears is float. Many large companies pay their employees on the West Coast with checks drawn on East Coast banks so that it can use the cash during the period that the check is written, cashed at a West Coast bank, shipped to an East Coast bank, and subtracted from the company's account. The following are additional examples of float:

1. *Disneyland Coupons.* Visitors to Disneyland exchange money for coupons at the gate. If they do not use all of the coupons in one day, they keep the rest for a return visit days, weeks, months (or never) in the future. Disneyland, of course, has been paid for the unusued coupons so that it gets float on the money.

2. *Traveler's Checks.* Bank of America, Citibank, Cooks, and American Express Company trade their traveler's checks for cash (the money you pay for the checks, if any, goes to the bank as a handling fee). The person who exchanges cash for traveler's checks takes a vacation, and periodically cashes the traveler's checks. Meanwhile, the issuing company has invested the cash it received. With a continuing stream of clients, the issuing company always has a substantial amount of float invested, earnings from which constitute the company's source of income.

3. *Trade Dollars.* A group of merchants wish to encourage business among themselves as a group. The promoters issue trade association dollars in exchange for real money. For as long as the trade dollars remain in circulation within the group, the promoters can benefit from the investment of the float.

4. *Gift Certificates.* Rather than purchase an item from a retail store, many people buy gift certificates for relatives and friends. Until the relatives and friends spend these certificates, however, the issuing company—the retailer—can use the money as float.

The above are examples of how float can be created. While most businesses do not create float, they can utilize it.

Bank reconciliations can be useful in developing statistical float data in addition to their usefulness in achieving agreement between the cash and the bank accounts. Float works two ways in a checking account: When deposits are made, a float of from two to three days is usually required before the checks clear the payor's accounts. This is "negative float"—until the deposits are cleared the firm may not issue checks or make withdrawals. On the other hand, checks issued by the firm are "float" until they have cleared the firm's bank account. This is "positive float." The difference between negative and positive float is "net negative" or "net positive" float. If the minimum float period is two days (based on mailing and clearing time), we can readily compute minimum float.

In addition, some suppliers may be in distant locations, or they may simply be slow depositors. To refine our measurement of float, we can analyze checks outstanding at the end of each month and "age" them according to various time periods shown:

Checks outstanding	0–30 days	31–60 days	61–90 days	Over 90 days
No. 1012				$500
1015			$1000	
1023			500	
1032		$1500		
1035		500		
1041	$ 500			
1046	2000			
1048	2500			
Total	$5000	$2000	$1500	$500

With sufficient aging data and experience, we have a basis for calculating probable float. You can calculate the percentage of total checks cashed in less than 30 days, less than 60 days, and so on. You could then figure that a certain amount of your checks are going to be outstanding, so that you could actually write checks for that percentage more than your cash balance in the bank. You could also get an idea of how long a certain company takes to cash checks. In this way float analysis can be a useful management cash control tool.

Receivables

Generally speaking, the term "receivables" indicates claims for money and goods due from other businesses. There are various types or categories of receivables, including:

- Accounts receivable (due from customers).
- Notes receivable (due from those who owe money and who have signed a negotiable instrument or note).
- Deposits receivable or returnable.
- Claims against various parties (governments, lawsuits).
- Advances to employees, officers, stockholders.

Current Versus Noncurrent Receivables. Receivables may be listed as current assets or as long-term assets. To be classified as a current asset, a receivable should be convertible into cash within one year's time, otherwise it should be classified as a noncurrent asset.

Receivables should be stated at their net realizable cash value. Initially, receivables may be stated at the invoice price of the sale if, for example, a credit sale for $100 is recorded. However, not all receivables are collectable; therefore, to state receivables at their net realizable cash value requires an estimate of the amounts of receivables that will not be collected. In other words, an allowance for bad debts or uncollectable accounts should be deducted from receivables. Estimating bad debt's allowances will be covered in a following section.

Bad Debts Expense. When you sell on credit, you must expect some customers not to pay. There are four principal methods of calculating estimates of bad debt expense:

- Percentage of sales (see Figure 5.4)
- Percentage of credit sales
- Percentage of outstanding receivables
- Aging receivables

Calculation of reserve for bad debts

Assume

Volume of charge sales	$1,000,000
Notes and accounts receivable	
Beginning of year	$ 80,000
End of year	$ 90,000

Amount of debts that have become wholly or partially worthless and have been charged against reserve account $ 2,500

Reserve for bad debts

Beginning	$ 2,700
Estimated percentage of bad debts	3%

Calculation of reserve

	Beginning	$2700
Less:	Charge-offs	(2500)
		$ 200
Add:	Addition to reserve	
	(3% × $1,000,000)	3000
Ending balance		$3200

Figure 5.4

All of these methods are currently in use. The percentage of credit sales and percentage of outstanding receivables are most commonly used. The aging method probably gives the most accurate figure for bad debts expense, and with increased use of computers it should become widely used.

Percentage of Credit Sales. When a percentage of sales approach is employed, a company's past experience with uncollectable accounts is analyzed. If there is a stable relationship between previous year's charge sales and bad debts, that relationship can be turned into a percentage and used to determine the current year's bad debt expense (see Figure 5.5).

Percentage of Outstanding Receivables. Using past experience, a company can estimate the percentage of its outstanding accounts receivables that will become uncollectable, without identifying specific accounts. This procedure provides a

Year	Credit Sales	Actual Bad Debts
19X3	$1,000,000	$15,000
19X2	900,000	12,000
19X1	800,000	12,000
Total	$2,700,000	$39,000

Percentage: $\dfrac{\$39,000}{2,700,000} = 1.44\%$

19X4 Credit sales: $1,200,000
19X4 Estimated bad debt expense: 1.44% × $1,200,000 = $17,280

Figure 5.5   Percentage of credit sales method of estimating bad debt expense.

Year	Accounts Receivable (End of Year)	Accounts Receivable That Become Bad Debts
19X3	$150,000	$15,000
19X2	140,000	12,000
19X1	135,000	12,000
TOTAL	$425,000	$39,000

Percentage: $\dfrac{\$39,000}{\$425,000} = 9.2\%$

19X4	Ending accounts receivable: $160,000
19X4	Estimated bad debt expense: $9.2\% \times \$160,000 = \$14,720$

Figure 5.6   Percentage of accounts receivable method of estimating bad debt expense.

reasonably accurate picture of the realizable value of the receivables at any time. It does not, however, match costs and revenues as well as the percentage of sales approach, because it relies on the past to predict the future (see Figure 5.6).

Aging of Accounts Receivable.   A more sophisticated approach than the percentage of outstanding receivables method is to set up an aging schedule. Such a schedule indicates which accounts require special attention by providing the age of the receivable (see Figure 5.7).

The amount $189 indicates the bad debt expense to be reported for the year, but only if this is the first year the company has been in operation. In subsequent years, the allowance for doubtful accounts balance is adjusted to the amount determined by the aging schedule. An aging schedule is not only prepared to determine bad debts

AGING SCHEDULE

Customer	Balance 12/31	Under 60 Days	61–90 Days	91–120 Days	Over 120 Days
Customer A	$1000	$ 800	$200		
Customer B	3000	3000			
Customer C	600				$600
Customer D	750	600		$150	
	$5350	$4400	$200	$150	$600

SUMMARY

Age	Amount	Percentage	
Under 60 days	$4400	1%	$ 44.00
61–90 days	200	5%	10.00
91–120 days	150	10%	15.00
Over 120 days	600	20%	120.00
Bad debts expense or allowance for doubtful accounts			$189.00

Figure 5.7

expense but it may also serve as a control device, to determine the composition of receivables and to identify delinquent accounts. The estimated loss percentage developed for each age category is based on previous loss experience and the advice of persons in your business who are responsible for granting credit.

Designing a Credit Policy. Receivables result from selling on credit, and the essence of credit sales lies in the trade-off between increased sales and increased collection costs. Credit sales can be increased indefinitely in most businesses simply by liberalizing credit agreements. However, the increased sales become unprofitable when the costs of collection exceed the profit margin. Therefore, a balance between increased sales and collection costs must be sought.

Credit rating services, such as Dun and Bradstreet and TRW Credit Data, are useful sources of data for making credit decisions, but rating services cannot make credit granting decisions. They only provide the historical background on a prospective customer.

In making a credit decision, an assessment of a customer's financial position and short-term liquidity is necessary. The most commonly used financial ratio for assessing short-term credit risk is the ratio of current assets to current liabilities. Based on recent research in the area of prediction of bankruptcy, a better ratio is cash flow to total debt.

Cash Flow to Debt Ratio. Cash flow is approximated by adding depreciation expense to net income and subtracting purchases of fixed assets and dividends. The ratio of cash flow to total debt will vary by industry, but a ratio of 1:4 may be an expected average (for public companies, the data is easily obtainable; for privately owned firms, the data will be sought by other means, principally by request of the potential customer).

Receivables Information System. A way to formulate a sound credit policy is to develop a credit information system, sometimes called a credit scoring system. This is based on the five C's of credit: character, capacity, capital, collateral, and conditions.

- *Character.* Defined as the probability that a client will try to honor his obligations, and measured by past payment history. Interviews and references can supply relevant information.
- *Capital.* Measured by the financial position of the firm as indicated by total assets, net worth, or debt to equity ratio.
- *Collateral.* Represented by assets the customer may offer as security.
- *Capacity.* Measured by the consistency of profitable operations.
- *Conditions.* The state of the economy and the state of the industry in which the customer operates.

An illustration of a credit scoring sheet appears in Figure 5.8.

How to Develop Credit Scores. Based on data supplied in the client's credit applications, assign points in each rating category, then decide a cut-off point. The sum of the points in each category provides the client's credit score (in the example in Figure 5.8), points range from 1 to 5, but you can set your own range to suit the facts of your industry.

As previously indicated, aging accounts is a useful technique, because it directs attention to the most troublesome areas, and it may indicate necessary changes in credit granting policy. If the data is available, another useful technique would be

Character					Points
Subjective measure points	Excellent	Good	Fair	Marginal	
	5	3	1	0	☐
Capacity					
Years of profit	15+	10–15	5–10	2–5	
	5	4	3	2	☐
Capital					
Debt/equity ratio	0–.10	.10–.25	.25–.80	.50–1.00	
	5	3	3	1	☐
Collateral					
Type	Mortgage	Securities	Pledge	None	
	5	4	2	1	☐
Conditions					
Sales growth in customer's industry	Growth in past four quarters	Growth in past two quarters	Stable	Decline	
	5	4	2	0	☐
Total score					☐

Figure 5.8.   Credit scoring chart.

analysis of payment history by customer class or category. Results of this technique may disclose that certain categories of customers are more trouble than they are worth, and that credit should either not be granted or granted only on restricted terms.

Payment Stimulation Techniques.   The essence of control over receivables is to minimize the amounts of money tied up in receivables while maximizing billing. Minimizing the investment in receivables may be facilitated by payment stimulation techniques. Ways to speed up the payment of receivables include:

- Discounts for early payment.
- Adding on interest for payment after a certain date.
- Dunning letters that become increasingly threatening as time passes.
- Personal telephone calls.
- Outside collection services.
- Legal action.

Clearly, you would like to stimulate payment with the method that costs least in terms of expense and customer alienation. There is a trade-off between the severity of the stimulation technique and maintenance of customer satisfaction. You should relate the severity of the technique to the age of the receivable.

By breaktime the instructor had covered a great deal of material—cash, cash management, and accounts receivable. He said that he wouldn't cover inventory that night because of the time limitations. After the break, he was going to discuss fixed assets and depreciation.

"Well," Lazarus Time said to Suzi Wo as they walked down to the snack bar, "This asset business has a lot to it. I don't even know how I can absorb all of these cash management techniques, much less set credit policy for accounts receivable."

"Yeah," Suzi replied. "Cash is the only important four-letter word in business." Suzi giggled. "My boss came in the other morning with this big grin on his face. And he's usually such a sourpuss. He had just gone on a selling trip. He said, 'I just found a great new source of cash—my customers.'"

NONCURRENT ASSETS

The primary category of noncurrent assets for most businesses is property, plant, and equipment, also referred to as *fixed assets*. Fixed assets are machines, desks, typewriters, buildings, trucks, and land. Virtually all businesses have fixed assets of some sort.

The interesting thing about fixed assets is that all of them except land are subject to depreciation. That is, fixed assets wear out from use at some point. Even apartment or office buildings, which seem to appreciate rather than depreciate in value, wear out at some point. Therefore, the Internal Revenue Code allows a deduction on all fixed assets for depreciation.

The remainder of this chapter will be concerned with depreciation. Depreciation, and the related topics of depletion and amortization, constitute one of the more important areas of accounting and taxation. As these words will be used frequently, they are defined here.

Depreciation. In accounting terms depreciation is defined as "the process of allocating against revenues the cost expiration of tangible property." Depreciation also carries the connotation of decline in value due to use or wear and tear.

Depletion. Depletion is defined as the process of allocating against revenue the cost expiration of an asset represented by a natural resource, such as an oil well.

Amortization. Amortization is defined as the process of allocating against revenue the cost expiration of intangibles represented by special rights such as patents or leaseholds.

In order to determine the amount of depreciation, depletion, or amortization to be recorded for a period, or to be deducted for tax purposes, it is essential to know first: (1) the cost of the asset, (2) the estimated economic useful life of the asset, and (3) the estimated salvage or residual value of the asset at the end of its useful life.

Example. If you purchase a machine for $11,000 and it has a five year economic life and an estimated salvage value of $1000, then using a straight-line depreciation method, you could record $2000 depreciation expense per year and deduct this amount against revenues and other income in calculating taxable income.

$$\frac{\$11,000 - \$1000}{5} = \$2000$$

Determining The Cost of an Asset

The acquisition cost of an asset is measured by the cash outlay made to acquire it. If something other than cash is exchanged for the asset, its fair market value at the time of the transaction will be the measure of cost. In the absence of a determinable fair market value for consideration given, the asset is recorded at *its* fair market value.

An asset is generally not considered to be acquired for accounting or tax purposes until it has been placed in the position where it is ready to be used and is suitable for production. Thus, all reasonable and legitimate costs incurred in placing an asset in service are considered to be part of the cost.

Cash Purchase. If an asset is purchased for cash, any outlay that "prudent buyer" would make for an asset, including costs of installation, should be capitalized. The capitalizable costs include the invoice price plus incidental costs, such as insurance during transit, freight, duties, title search, registration fees, and installation costs.

Credit Purchases. If an asset is acquired on a deferred payment basis, the cash equivalent price of the asset, excluding interest, should be capitalized. Actual or imputed interest on the debt incurred to buy the asset is considered an expense when it is paid or accrued. Even if the purchase contract does not specify interest on the liability, "imputed interest" should be deducted in determining the cost of the asset.

Example. To illustrate the purchase of an asset on credit, assume your company purchased a machine under a contract that required equal payments of $3154.70 at the end of each of four years when the prevailing interest rate was 10% per annum. To record the asset as $12,618.80 ($3154.70 × 4) would include interest in the cost of the asset. The actual cost of the asset is the present value of the four payments discounted at 10%.

$$Purchase\ value = annual\ payment \times present\ value\ of\ an\ annuity$$
$$= \$3,154.70 \times 3.1699$$
$$= \$10,000$$

Therefore, the cost of the machine would be $10,000. Likewise, the difference between the $10,000 cost and the total of the installment payments ($12,618.80) represents *interest expense* which may be deducted as it is paid.

Assets Acquired by Exchange for Stocks or Bonds. If assets are acquired in exchange for stocks, the determination of cost may be difficult to achieve. This is because there may be no readily determinable fair market value for the stocks or the assets involved. Also, the assets may have been transferred to the business in exchange for stock. This is often a "related party transaction," where the owners of the company are contributing assets to the company. The value or cost of both the acquired asset and the associated stock or notes is difficult to determine. As a consequence, the *Internal Revenue Code* typically indicates that, where assets are transferred to a corporation or a partnership in exchange for ownership interests, the cost basis of the asset will be the same for the corporation as it was for the transferror/stockholder.

Assets Acquired in Exchange for Other Assets. If assets are acquired in exchange for other assets, further problems arise regarding the determination of the cost of the acquired assets. Items of property, plant, and equipment are frequently acquired by trading in an old asset in full—or part—payment for another asset. In some cases an asset is acquired by exchanging another asset plus payment of receipt of cash. Cash paid or received in an exchange transaction is often referred to as "boot."

For tax purposes, the cost of an asset acquired through an exchange is equal to the cost of the asset given up, plus any cash boot given.

Example. If your company acquired an automobile three years ago for $9000 that has an estimated life of six years, with no salvage value, and it used straight line depreciation, then the current *book value*, or *basis*, of the truck would be $4500:

$$\$9,000 \div 6 \text{ years} = \$1500$$
$$3 \text{ years} \times (\$1500 = \$4,500$$

If you traded in the old auto for a new auto, and paid $3000 cash in addition, you would then have a new auto with a book value, or basis, for accounting and tax depreciation purposes of $7,500, despite the fact that the new auto might have a list price higher or lower than that amount:

$$\begin{array}{r} \$4500 \\ +\ \ 3000 \\ \hline \$7500 \end{array}$$

Investment Tax Credit

It is important to determine the cost of an asset not only for depreciation purposes, but also for the *investment tax credit*. The investment tax credit was established by Congress in order to stimulate the purchase of machinery and equipment throughout the economy. It was first created in 1962 and has been modified subsequently several times. An investment credit is allowed against your tax liability when certain qualified business property is placed into service. The credit may also apply to progress payments made during the course of building or acquiring qualified property. The credit has *no effect* on regular depreciation.

Taxpayers can take a 10% credit directly off taxes due for investments in qualified business property acquired after January 2, 1975.

Example. A consulting firm spends $30,000 to purchase leasehold improvements and furniture. The company conservatively estimates that the improvements and furniture will last seven years. Since the life is seven years, the firm qualified for the full 10% income tax credit. Ten percent of $30,000 is $3000. After the firm has calculated its taxes due for the years, it can subtract $3000 from the total.

A corporate taxpayer may elect an 11% credit in an amount equal to 1% of the investment if it is contributed to an *employee stock ownership plan*. The maximum amount of credit that can be taken in any one taxable year is $50,000, plus half of its tax liability in excess of $50,000. This limitation will not affect most individuals or corporations, but for large corporations with large investments, there may have to be a deferral of the use of the credit to future tax years. The credit can be deferred up to seven years.

Example. A company's tax liability—the amount of taxes they were to pay before the investment tax credit—is $100,000. The maximum credit allowable is $75,000 ($50,000 plus half of the remaining $50,000). If they buy qualified property costing $200,000, their credit would be $20,000 and their tax liability would be $80,000. Depreciation would be calculated on the basis of $200,000.

The amount of qualified investment depends on the *useful life* of the property to which the credit applies. It is determined from the cost of used or new property. This is why the cost of an asset, as discussed previously, is quite important.

Example.   If you trade in a machine with a book value of $4000 and pay an additional $1000 cash for a new machine, the cost of the new machine would be $5000, and you would be allowed an investment credit of $500 (10% of $5000).

However, if the machine you acquire is *used,* rather than new, then only the excess cost above the book value qualifies for the investment credit. Therefore, in the example above, your investment credit would be reduced to $100 (10% of $5000 − $4000). The reduction in the investment credit for used property has no effect on depreciation. You can still depreciate $5000 of cost over the life of the acquired machine.

The rule about used property applies even if you sell an asset and then later reinvest the proceeds in a used asset of a similar type. For example; if you sell an auto that has a book value of $3000, and then later you buy an auto for $5000, the amount of cost that qualifies for the investment credit is limited to $2000.

The investment tax credit applies to *depreciable tangible personal property*, which means it applies to property used in your trade or business which has a physical existence and which is not inventory, supplies, or real estate.

Examples of qualified property include office equipment, machinery in a factory, computers in a store, and neon signs for advertising. Even the cost of producing a motion picture or television film has been considered to be qualified property though it is more intangible than tangible. Some costs that are ordinarily considered to be costs of real property qualify for the investment credit if the real property is used as an integral part of a manufacturing, mining, or utility type of facility.

The investment credit also applies to real property in certain circumstances. In order to qualify, the real property must be an integral part of a manufacturing, production, mining, or utility operation, or it must constitute a research facility or a facility for bulk storage of commodities. Examples of real property qualifying for the investment credit include blast furnaces, oil derricks, oil and gas pipelines, broadcasting towers, and railroad tracks.

The credit is allowed for the year that the qualifying property is placed into service. This is the earlier of either the first year that depreciation on the asset can be taken, or the year the asset becomes ready for its intended purpose.

There is a limit on the amount of investment in used property and equipment that will qualify for the investment tax credit. The limit is $100,000 for both corporations and individuals. However, if you are married and file a separate tax return, the limit is $50,000. For a partnership, the limitation is $100,000 for the partnership as a whole.

Income Tax Credit Exclusions.   No investment credit is allowed for property with a useful life of *less* than three years. Used property will not be qualified if, after you acquire it, it is used by the person from whom you acquired it. An example of this might be a sale and lease-back arrangement. Property which you have used before or property you repossessed will not qualify. Property which you acquire from your subsidiary, or from your parent company if you are a more than 50% owned subsidiary, would not qualify. If you sell or give personally owned property to a business which you control, the business cannot take a credit.

No credit is allowed for property that is used primarily for housing or to provide lodging, such as a hotel or motel. However, facilities related to housing or lodging may qualify, such as a restaurant in a hotel, or laundry machines in an apartment building.

Useful Life Limitations.   In order to qualify for the full investment credit, the useful life of the asset must be at least seven years. If the useful life is five or six years, then only two thirds of the cost of the asset qualifies for the credit. If the useful life is three or four years, then only one third of the cost qualifies. If the useful life is less than three years, the asset does not qualify for the credit.

Example.   Assume that you purchase a delivery truck, a small computer and a lathe.

Asset	Years of useful life	Cost	Percentage	Qualified amount
Delivery truck	3	$ 9,000	33⅓	$ 3,000
Computer	5	12,000	66⅔	8,000
Lathe	7	15,000	100	15,000
				$26,000

Investment credit ($26,000 × 10%) = $2600

If the credit is not used in the period when it is earned, it may be carried back to offset taxes paid up to three years previously, and may be carried forward up to seven years. Investment tax credits carried forward from previous years are used to reduce your current taxes before credits earned in the current year.

The investment credit may have to be recaptured if the asset is not held at least seven years. Even if the asset is destroyed, recapture of the credit will occur.

Example.   If you bought a machine in 1978 which has a useful life of ten years and cost $8,000, and in 1978 you could have taken an $800 credit. However, if the machine is destroyed by fire in 1980, the $800 will be added to your tax liability for 1980.

Depreciation

Once you have acquired a depreciable asset and have determined its cost, then the question of depreciation arises.

The Internal Revenue Code recognizes that a depreciation allowance is necessary because property gradually approaches a point when its usefulness is exhausted. Therefore, depreciation is allowed only on property that has a definitely limited useful life. Depreciation may even be allowed on fruit trees if it can be shown that the trees have a limited life.

Intangible property can be depreciated if its use in a business is of limited duration. Examples of depreciable intangibles include licenses, franchises, patents, and copyrights. Ordinarily depreciation of intangibles is referred to as amortization.

Depreciation Methods.   The Internal Revenue Code specifies three particular methods of computing depreciaiton. However, others may be used. The three methods are:

1. Straight line
2. Declining balance
3. Sum of the years digits

You do not need to use the same method for all your depreciable property, but once you choose a method for a particular property you must continue using that method unless you obtain approval from the Internal Revenue Service to change methods.

Obtaining approval to change is not a problem. You simply file Form 3115 during the first 180 days of the year of the change.

Useful Life.   You may enter into an agreement with the IRS as to the useful life, depreciation method, and salvage value of any property. However, there are classes of property that have been established by Internal Revenue Regulations. These classes each have *asset depreciation ranges.* If you choose a useful life within the limits of the asset depreciation range for a given asset, you will not be challenged by the IRS.

Salvage value, established at the point when property is acquired, is the amount that can be realized when the property is no longer useful to the taxpayer. Salvage value may be no more than junk value, or it may be a large portion of the original cost, depending on the length of time before the end of the asset's useful economic life. Useful economic life is determined by when the taxpayer plans to dispose of the asset. An estimated salvage value of *less than* 10% of original cost may be *disregarded* in computing depreciation. However, no asset may be depreciated below a reasonable salvage value.

Salvage value must be subtracted from original cost in computing straight line and sum of the years digits depreciation. It is *not* subtracted in computing declining balance depreciation.

Example.   A consulting firm purchased leasehold improvements for $30,000 which have a salvage value of $9000 and a useful life of seven years. The first year of depreciation under each of the three methods is as follows:

Straight Line: $30,000 minus $9000 divided by seven = $3000

Sum of the Years Digits: $30,000 minus $9000 times 7/28 = $5250

Double Declining Balance: $30,000 times 0.2857 = $8571

Straight Line.   The formula for straight line depreciation is: Cost minus salvage value divided by useful life equals depreciation for each year.

Sum of the Years Digits.   Sum of the years digits depreciation allocates a declining portion of the total cost to depreciation expense in each year. In the example shown above where leasehold improvements were purchased for $30,000 and had a salvage value of $9000 and a useful life of seven years, sum of the years digits depreciation would be calculated as follows:

Year	Factor	×	Cost minus salvage	=	Depreciation expense
1	7/28		$21,000		$ 5,250
2	6/28		21,000		4,500
3	5/28		21,000		3,750
4	4/28		21,000		3,000
5	3/28		21,000		2,250
6	2/28		21,000		1,500
7	1/28		21,000		750
					$21,000

A useful formula for calculating the denominator of the sum of the years digits fraction is:

$$\frac{n\,(n\,+\,1)}{2}$$

where n = useful life

Example.

$$\text{Useful life} = 7 \text{ years}$$

$$\frac{7 \times 8}{2} = 28$$

Declining Balance.   The declining balance method applies a constant percentage to the declining book value of the asset.

Example.   Assume that the cost of machine is \$30,000, and its useful life is seven years.

Year	Percentage	×	Book value	=	Annual depreciation
1	28.57%		\$30,000		\$ 8,571
2	28.57%		21,429		6,122
3	28.57%		15,307		4,373
4	28.57%		10,934		3,124
5	28.57%		7,810		2,231
6	28.57%		5,579		1,594
7	28.57%		3,985		1,138
					\$27,153

Note.   In the double declining balance calculation above the total depreciation (which is \$27,153) exceeds the original cost (\$30,000) minus salvage value (\$9000) of \$21,000. This would *not* be allowed for tax purposes. Since the tax people only allow you \$21,000 worth of depreciation, only \$1,934 in depreciation could be taken in the Fourth year and no depreciation could be taken in the fifth, sixth, and seventh. This is because the first three years' depreciation comes to \$19,066, leaving only \$1934 (\$21,000 minus \$19,066) for the balance of the depreciation.

The maximum rate on declining balance depreciation is specified by the following table. The factor is multiplied by the straight line rate in order to find the maximum declining balance rate.

Type of property	Factor
New equipment	2
Used equipment	1½
New real estate	1½
Used real estate	1
Used residential rental property	1¼

Example.   You buy a new apartment building with a 50 year useful life. The maximum percentage you can use on declining balance depreciation is 3% (1½ × 1/50).

Sum of the years digits cannot be used for real estate, except for new residential rental buildings such as apartment houses.

Usually when you acquire an asset during a year, you prorate the depreciation that you owe on the asset.

Example.   On April 1, you acquire a machine for $12,000 which has a useful life of 10 years. You decide to use straight line depreciation. The depreciation expense for the year of acquisition would be $900 ($12,000 ÷ 10 × 9/12).

Gains and Losses on Sales.   The rules regarding the computation of gains and losses upon sale or retirement of depreciable assets are somewhat complicated. In general, capital gains and losses are taxed at different rates than gains and losses on the sale of other assets. Depreciable property has been determined not to be a capital asset, therefore, capital gains and losses are not allowable when depreciable property is sold. However, Congress decided (Section 1231 of the Internal Revenue Code) to extend capital gain treatment to depreciable assets while preserving the benefits of ordinary loss treatment. Later, Congress changed its mind and added Section 1245 of the Code which provides that for equipment which you sell, you have ordinary gain treatment to the extent of any depreciation taken on the equipment.

Example 1.   You buy a machine in 1978 for $10,000 and decide to depreciate it on the straight line method over ten years. By the end of 1980 you have taken $2000 in depreciation. If you then sell the machine for $11,000, you must record $2000 of ordinary income gain and $1000 of capital gain.

Example 2.   On January 1, 1971 you bought a machine for $6000. You claimed $600 depreciation on it for each year and sold it for $2000 on July 1, 1980. Your adjusted basis on the date of sale was $300 ($6000 less $5700 which represents $600 per year depreciation between 1971 and 1980—9 years—plus $300 for the half year in 1980). Therefore, your gain was $1700 on the sale. Since the gain ($1700) was less than the total depreciation ($5700), the entire gain must be included as ordinary income.

On *real property*, gain or loss is calculated in the same way as personal property if the following applies: (1) You compute depreciation on the property using the straight-line method (or any other method resulting in depreciation not in excess of that computed by the straight-line method), and you have held the property more than a year; (2) You realize a loss on the sale of property; Otherwise, real property disposal by sale or exchange must be calculated by a special formula to determine what portion of the gain is to be treated as ordinary income.

When the class had ended, Lazarus's head was clicking like a Geiger counter. "Man," he thought, "there is just a lot to this asset business. You've got the current assets like cash and accounts receivable around which all the business's cash planning evolves. And then there's noncurrent assets. Now there the trick seems to be to buy things like machinery, so that you can get the maximum tax benefits through income tax credit and depreciation. But what does an asset cost? Determining what the asset costs seems to have a lot to do with whether it was bought on time, traded for, or bought outright with cash. . .".

Deep in thought, Laz heard someone speak to him. It was Suzi Wo. "Can you help me with a question?" she asked.

"Sure."

"What is the difference between bookkeeping and accounting? Do you know?" Suzi asked.

Lazarus paused for a minute to think. He thought about what he and Ignatz were doing at W.T. Technologies. That was obviously bookkeeping. What the instructor was talking about tonight was clearly accounting. "Well, I think it is all accounting. I mean it's all *technically* called accounting. Keeping track of the original documents like checks is bookkeeping. Determining the value of an asset or determining what is the best depreciation, that's accounting. I think the borderline between accounting and bookkeeping is determined by whether or not you have to apply an intrepreta-tion of the law. When it comes to intrepretation of tax laws and practices—that's accounting."

Suzi Wo looked up at Laz and asked "Are you sure?"

Chapter Six
Liabilities and Loans

The more Lazarus Time worked on the books making entries, the more he realized that W.T. Technologies was going to need a loan. W.T. had backlogged a few of their machines, and the machines weren't sold. Producing for inventory can be expensive, especially considering the length of time that his customers were waiting to pay. He was glad that the instructor was going to talk about loans that night.

W.T. Technologies right now only had two major liabilities—the amount they owed their suppliers and the amount the company owed Ignatz Whiz for his officer's loan. Laz had wanted to pay off Whiz's loan, but their sales had been so small and their expenses were high. Actually, Laz never expected that the accounts payable would get so out of hand either.

Laz had a lot of questions for the instructor that night if the material wasn't covered in the lecture. He wanted to find out what types of loans were available, how much he could borrow, and when the best and worst times to borrow were. He had heard about special loans from the United States government, and he thought it would be nice to find out about that, too.

The teacher was standing at the head of the class when Laz entered the classroom. He was wearing a bright orange shirt and a pair of Levi cords that were too short. He began. . . .

Liabilities are the amounts your company owes. Liabilities are obligations that result from past transactions and require you to pay with assets (cash), or render services, in the future. Liabilities are usually definite in amount, or subject to reasonable estimation. The amounts are stated or implied in oral or written contracts.

Liabilities can be classified into current and noncurrent. *Current liabilities* are those which are due and payable within one year. They include such things as salaries and wages payable; other accrued expenses, such as for utilities, taxes and supplies; accounts payable for inventories; and short term notes payable to banks and others.

Salaries and wages payable and other accrued expenses are really another side of expenses and cash disbursements. We have previously discussed cash disbursements arising from operating expenses. The main thing to remember with accrued expenses is to keep track of cash disbursements by using a check register and cash disbursements journal.

The other current liabilities typically represent debt due to banks and others, and are usually documented by a note. A note is a form of I.O.U. and is usually a legal document. This means that the holder of the note can take it to a court in order to have its provisions enforced.

Noncurrent liabilities are those which are due and payable in more than one year's time. Noncurrent liabilities are also referred to as *long-term debt*. Nearly all long-term debt is evidenced by a note. So notes pertain to both long-term and short-term debt.

DEBT

Every business in the United States regardless of size must from time to time borrow money. Usually a business will borrow from a bank, but it may also borrow from commercial finance companies; state, local and federal governments; and the public bond market. The larger the business, the more likely that it can tap all of these debt sources. The smaller the business, the more likely that it will only be able to use banks, government, and commercial loan sources.

Because this chapter of necessity is limited in scope, we shall not discuss publicly issued bonds. This is a speciality operation that requires accountants, lawyers and underwriters. Moreover, most businesses in the United States will never be in a position to sell public bonds. We will limit our discussion to the traditional sources of debt capital: banks, commercial financial lenders, and government (such as Small Business Administrations loans).

This chapter will offer a discussion of financial leverage, the types of loans that are available from the different sources, the physical requirements of loan applications, and the accounting implications of debt financing.

FINANCIAL LEVERAGE

Financial leverage is usually defined as the ratio of total debt to total assets. For example, a firm having assets of $1 million and total debt of $500,000 has a leverage factor of 50% ($500,000 ÷ $1,000,000).

The best way to understand the proper use of financial leverage is to analyze its impact on profitability under varying conditions. Let's take the example of three firms in the electronic supply industry that are identical except for their debt percentage. Yourcompany has used no debt and consequently has a leverage factor of zero. Hiscompany has financed their firm half by debt and half by equity so they have a leverage factor of 50%. Theircompany has a leverage factor of 75%. The companies' balance sheets are shown in Figure 6.1.

How a company's *capitalization* affects stockholder returns depends on the state of the economy in the industry. Let us assume that when the economy is depressed the

		Yourcompany	
		Total debt	$-0-
		Net worth	$100
Total assets	$100	Total liability and worth	$100
		Hiscompany	
		Total debt	$ 50
		Net worth	$ 50
Total assets	$100	Total liability and worth	$100
		Theircompany	
		Total debt @ 8%	$ 75
		Net worth	$ 25
Total assets	$100	Total liability and worth	$100

Figure 6.1

firms can earn 4% on assets because sales and profit margins are low. When the economy is brighter, the firms can earn 8%. Under normal conditions they will earn 11%, 15% under good conditions, and a 20% rate of return on assets if the economy is very good. The table in Figure 6.2 illustrates how the use of financial leverage magnifies the impact on stockholders (or firm owners) and relates directly to changes in the rate of return on assets.

As shown in the illustrations, when economic conditions go from normal to good, return on assets for Yourcompany (no leverage) goes up 36.4%, return on equity for Hiscompany (50% leverage) increase 57.1%, and return on equity for Theircompany (75% leverage) goes up a full 80%. Just the reverse happens when the economy is depressed. When the economy drops from normal to poor, Yourcompany's return on equity declines only 27%; whereas Hiscompany, which has a higher leverage has a decline in return on equity of 42.9%; and Theircompany, which has the highest leverage shows a decline in return on equity of a full 60%. In other words, the companies with the highest leverage (most debt as a percentage of total assets) receive the best return for owner's capital in normal or good times, but the worst return on equity in depressed economic times. The companies with the least leverage (least debt as a percentage of total assets) reap the highest relative return in times of a depressed economy.

	Very Poor	Poor	Normal	Good	Very Good
Rate of return on total assets before interest	4%	8%	11%	15%	20%
Dollar return on total assets before interest	$4	$8	$11	$15	$20
Yourcompany: No Leverage					
Earnings in dollars	$4	8	11	15	20
Less: Interest expense	$0	0	0	0	0
Gross income	$4	8	11	15	20
Taxes (50%)*	$2	4	5.5	7.5	10
Available to owners	$2	4	5.5	7.5	10
Percentage return on equity	2%	4%	5.5%	7.5%	10%
Hiscompany: Leverage 50%					
Earnings in dollars	$4	8	11	15	20
Less: Interest expense	$4	4	4	4	4
Gross income	$0	4	7	11	16
Taxes (50%)*	$0	2	3.5	5.5	8
Available to owners	$0	2	3.5	5.5	8
Percentage return on equity	0%	4%	7%	11%	16%
Theircompany: Leverage 75%					
Earnings in dollars	$4	8	11	15	20
Less: Interest expense	$6	6	6	6	6
Gross income	$(2)	2	5	9	14
Taxes (50%)*	$(1)	1	2.5	4.5	7
Available to owners	$(1)	1	2.5	4.5	7
Percentage return on equity	–4%	4%	10%	18%	28%

*The tax calculation assumes tax credits for losses.

Figure 6.2   Economic conditions.

As one would expect, wide variations on the use of financial leverage may be observed among industries and among the individual firms in each industry. Financial institutions use the most leverage. Financial institutions typically have high liabilities. Public utility use of debt stems from a heavy fixed asset investment, coupled with extremely stable sales. Mining and manufacturing firms use relatively less debt because of their exposure to fluctuating sales. Small firms as a group are heavy users of debt.

In the manufacturing industries, wide variations in leverage are observed for individual industries. The lowest debt ratios are found in textile manufacturing because their competitive pressures tend to be great. Low debt ratios are also found in the durable goods industries. The highest reliance on debt is found in consumer nondurable goods industries where demand is relatively insensitive to fluctuations in general business activity.

SOURCES OF DEBT CAPITAL

Not counting public debt offerings, there are basically three sources for debt capital: banks, commercial/finance companies, and government agencies.

Banks

The advantages of securing a bank loan are:

1. Generally, with the exception of a few government and private programs, borrowing from a bank is the least expensive way to borrow.
2. Borrowing from a bank, as opposed to a government or commercial source, is usually better for your credit rating.
3. Banks have the largest loan breadth, that is, more types of loans, and more sources.
4. Banks offer many business services, including credit references on customers or potential customers of your business: financial, investment, and estate advisory services; discounting services for customers' accounts and notes payable; safe deposit boxes; night depositories.

The disadvantages of dealing with banks include:

1. The financially conservative nature of banks may cause difficulties; that is, bank loans are the most difficult of the loans to obtain.
2. In banks that have a large number of branches, there is a tendency to have a branch manager work at one branch for only a couple of years; therefore it is difficult to set up a long-term relationship with that branch manager.
3. The technical requirements (financial spreads, projected budgets, corporate and ownership information, etc.) of presenting a loan application are greater with a bank than with other sources.
4. Because banks are regulated by the federal government, and are simultaneously profit-making organizations, they have to be careful their loans do not fail. For most long-term loans, banks demand annual, semi-annual, quarterly, or even monthly income statements and balance sheets so that they can observe your business carefully. Remember, they have the records of every check you have ever written.

What is the best time and the worst time to approach a bank for money? Of course, depending on your personal or company situation, any time might be a good time or bad time, irrespective of external influences and bank policies. That is, you might fall into the category of what we call the unwritten golden rule of borrowing, which says: "If you don't need money, that's the best time to get a loan."

On an external basis (i.e., having to do with the bank and the economy only), the following are the best times and situations in which to borrow:

1. When interest rates are generally low. This means two things, that the bank has more money to loan than it usually does and that the borrower will get a better deal.

2. When a bank has just opened. New banks, especially independent banks, are looking for business, especially deposit business. Newly opened banks will take more chances with a marginal business because they have to build up their loan portfolios. Sometimes you will find that new banks are conservative, but if you start building a relationship immediately, and you don't ask for a loan at the start, the bank will loan to you when they get to know you. Incidentally, if you have a sizable business, banking with a small independent will be good because you might be their biggest depositor. If you are, they will bend over backwards to give you service.

3. When the economy is in an up-turn. That is, when sales all over the economy are increasing, the stock market is up, and disposable consumer income is up. This might be reflected in lower interest rates, but not necessarily.

4. When banks in a particular area are in heavy competition. This might mean that there are too many banks in a new, developing area. You can tell there is a lot of competition if more than one bank visits your business to start up a relationship (the more, the better for you). Another sign is if there are a lot of incentives for deposits. That is, banks are trying to outdo themselves in the premiums (toasters, calculators, etc.) they offer for deposits.

5. When banks are in a generally expansionary process. During the 1960s, banks downplayed their traditional conservatism and started expanding their branch systems—including international branches—tremendously. Since there was more competition and a downgrading of traditional restraints, money was easier to obtain. There is a new facet of banking that might spark expansion: electronic banking devices called consumer-bank communication terminals, or CBCTs. These are the electronic devices that banks put outside their branches, or in supermarkets, shopping centers, and so on. These devices provide money or allow you to deposit without ever going to the bank. If the use of these devices becomes widespread, then the banks that get the most deposits will have mre money to loan.

6. When there is a special program within a bank—usually a large bank—to take high-risk loans as "the bank's moral obligation." Examples of this are loans to minorities, to special groups like veterans, the handicapped, and, in some cases, displaced businesses or disaster victims. The large banks sometimes set aside sums for these "special high-risk" loans; but beware, regardless of the bank's good intentions, if the economy is bad or there is a high demand on loan funds, these special loans have a way of being forced out.

The worst times and situations for borrowing are:

1. When interest rates are high. When rates are high it means that there is a large demand on bank funds, in many cases from large, secure "Fortune 500" type

firms. Also, at these times, a bank might have reached its loan limit according to its loan to deposit ratio (discussed shortly). High interest rates mean not only that money is more expensive, but also that there is less of it to borrow.

2. When the economy is in a recession. In recessionary times, regardless of other influences, banks tend to be more conservative in their lending. There are more chances for a business to go under in a recession. Furthermore, there is usually high demand for money to tide an established business over.

3. When a bank is up to its lending limit, or when the bank has made a decision to decrease its dollars outstanding to make the bank more liquid. When there is an extremely high demand for funds, the bank is tempted to loan at high rates and therefore make a better profit. There is a limit to how much money they can loan out, however, and that limit is their maximum loan-to-deposit ratio. The loan-to-deposit ratio is simply the total number loans they have outstanding divided by the total number of deposits they have. During 1974, the banks sometimes loaned out up to 75% of their deposits. This was difficult for the banks because if only 26% of their depositors took out their money, these banks would be in serious trouble, perhaps bankruptcy. Even this 75% loan-to-deposit ratio might be misleading. Banks have to report their loan-to-deposit ratio to the federal governm hours to bring up their deposits to help the ratio. In the early part of the twentieth century, the banks would very seldom go above 33% loan-to-deposit ratio. Thus, 75% is a thin edge to walk on.

   In 1975, when money supplies increased, loans did not. The reason was that although more money was available to loan out, the banks wanted to keep the money to build up their loan-to-deposit ratio and make the ratio healthier.

4. When there is very little bank competition for loans and deposits. A one bank town is a perfect example. When you need money, you go there—there is no competition. The best thing to do in this situation is to go to another town for financing.

5. When the bank is in trouble or suffers severe losses. In 1973, when United California Bank had trouble with its Swiss subsidiary, it was very difficult to get financing from the branches. If you read the business section of your newspaper, the *Wall Street Journal*, *Business Week*, or other business publications, you may learn if your bank is having troubles.

Of course, it is not always possible to wait for the right time to get a loan, and chances are good you will need money the most when everyone else need it.

Commercial Lenders

Commercial lenders, including commercial finance companies (factors, industrial time sales, leases), life insurance companies, foundations, and other private financial companies, are usually more expensive to borrow from than banks, but they make more loans to a broader class of customers than banks.

Commercial lenders, in general, are willing to loan to businesses that are not as strong financially as the businesses that banks would consider. Furthermore, commercial lenders are willing to take as collateral items which banks would be more selective about, such as inventories and receivables. In short, the major advantage of commercial lenders is their flexibility.

The major disadvantage of commercial lenders is that their interest rates are generally higher—sometimes much higher—than banks.

Life insurance companies, pension funds, and foundations offer money to business for real estate, equipment, and sometimes working capital, in amounts that are usually greater than the typical bank loans. Their interest rates are usually only slightly higher than those of banks. The disadvantage of these companies is that they usually only make large loans (in excess of $1 million) and require the applicant companies to be financially strong. This generally eliminates most small business from consideration.

Government Loans

The largest single lender to business in the United States is the federal government, followed by state and local governments. The federal government's lending program is larger than the loan programs of Bank of America, Chase Manhattan, Citibank, Morgan Guaranty Trust, and the rest of the ten largest banks in America. The United States government loans over $1.9 trillion per year to business.

Without question, the cheapest loans available in this country are those made by the government. Unfortunately, only a few special businesses, under very special circumstances, qualify for these loans. Most businesses, however, do qualify for government loans that have interest at a few points over prime. Although most government loans carry interest rates that are the same as or a little higher than bank rates, the government will make loans to businesses with higher risk than the banks. For instance, a start-up business that requires $100,000 in capital and has only $35,000 would not qualify for a loan at a bank at *any* interest rate. The same business, however, would qualify for a Small Business Administration (SBA) loan at near bank interest rates.

The equity requirements for most government loans are also less than those of a bank. For a start-up business, banks usually require 50% equity, whereas government loans require from 10 to 45% equity. For instance, let us take the example of a person who wants to start a business and has $15,000 in cash. At the bank he would be eligible for a maximum loan of another $15,000, for a total of $30,000. If the same person applied for a government loan, he could receive $18,300 to $150,000, depending on the loan program. Starting a business with $45,000 instead of $30,000 can make a big difference in the long-range success of that business.

The repayment period for government loans is also usually longer than the repayment period for bank loans. For this reason, your monthly payment as a businessperson is usually lower with a government loan than with a bank loan. For example, if a business borrows $10,000 for three years (bank average) at 10.25%, the monthly payments are $323.85. If on the other hand, the same firm borrows the same amount ($10,000) at the same interest rate (10.25%) for *seven* years instead of three years, the monthly payments are $167.31, or $165.54 less than the three year loan.

Along with the advantages of government loans there are some significant disadvantages. Government loans and government guaranteed loans take from three months to three years to receive approval. The effort required in paperwork and research is four times as great as a bank loan and twice as great as a commercial loan. In short, the greatest disadvantages of government loans are the time required for approval and the paperwork involved.

TYPES OF LOANS AVAILABLE FROM BANKS, COMMERCIAL AND GOVERNMENT LENDERS

The following is a listing of the types of loans that are available to the businessperson and a brief discussion of the type of financing where each is used.

Bank Loans

Loans that are from 30 to 90 days are called *short-term loans*. Short-term loans are usually employed to finance inventory on which a business can expect to get a cash return in a short period of time. New businesses very seldom receive short-term loans because most new businesses cannot turn their money around during the first few months of operations. However, short-term loans are used extensively for existing businesses.

Intermediate term loans are for more than one year, but less than five years. Equipment loans fall into this category. Most businesses that request a bank loan will receive this type of loan unless they are financing property or getting a government guaranteed loan. A person who plans to buy an existing business and borrow money on a regular bank loan will probably obtain a loan with a term of from three to five years.

Long-term loans are for periods of five years or more. Government guaranteed loans are usually for more than five years. Banks will also make long-term loans for improvements and property.

Term loans are further classified into secured and unsecured loans. *Secured loans* require security: a businessperson must pledge some physical thing of value as security or collateral for the money the bank loans. A loan for buying equipment is a secured loan, because equipment is pledged as security which the bank can repossess in the event the borrower is unable to make the payments. *Unsecured loans* have no collateral pledged. Unsecured loans are made on "your good name," that is, on the strength of your credit in general, and in particular on your credit with the bank that makes the loan.

Only the rare businessperson getting started or attempting extensive expansion will obtain an unsecured loan. Even government guaranteed loans are "partially secured" (not totally supported by collateral, but supported with collateral to a large extent).

Secured loans fall into three categories: loans secured by liquid assets (stocks, bonds, or cash), loans secured by accounts receivable, and loans secured by fixed assets (equipment, improvements, and property).

Liquid asset loans are loans that use savings accounts, stocks, or bonds for collateral. Usually with this kind of loan the business leaves its stock, bonds, or savings with the bank and the bank loans an amount equal to (for savings) or less than (with stocks and bonds whose market value fluctuates) the amount of the security. The advantage of this type of loan is that the interest rate charged is cheap (1 to 2% over what you are earning on savings, or near prime in the case of stocks or bonds).

Accounts receivable secured loans, including both factoring and accounts receivables financing, are not available to a business just starting out. Accounts receivable financing—and more especially factoring—tends to be an expensive way to finance a business. This type of financing is best used in a situation where sales are growing faster than cash flow. In accounts receivable financing (which has cheaper interest than factoring), the lender loans up to 80% of the value of your receivables (assuming all the accounts are reasonably good). The customer pays the firm and the firm brings the endorsed check to the lender. In factoring, the lender buys the firm's accounts. When a factor buys receivables, the customer pays the factor directly and receives a statement stating that the account is owned by that factor.

Fixed Asset secured loans are for large "capital" items like equipment, land and buildings, improvements, and fixtures. Fixed asset loans are usually for the longest period of all the secured loans discussed so far. Real estate loans are a good example of secured fixed asset loans. All fixed assets loans are for terms of at least two years and usually exceed five years in length.

Government guaranteed loans should interest most businessmen. For the vast majority of beginning small business, the best government guaranteed loan is the Small Business Administration (SBA) guaranteed loan. The SBA loan guarantees the bank 90% against loss. That means that when you borrow $100,000 from a bank with an SBA guarantee, if you lose all the money in the first week, the bank will be paid 90% of the loss, or $90,000 by the SBA. The SBA guaranteed loan is for high risk types of business—that is, small, and especially new, businesses. The borrower has to meet other requirements; information is available from local SBA offices. In most cases, however, small and new "start-up" businesses qualify.

Commercial Finance Companies

Types of loans available from commercial finance companies include: equipment and fixture loans (including commercial time financing); accounts receivable loans (including accounts receivable financing); and equipment leasing (leasing companies). The types of loans will be covered in that order:

Equipment loans. These loans include basically two types: money loaned against presently owned equipment, and money loaned to finance new equipment and financed on a time sales financing basis.

Commercial finance companies will sometimes make loans on presently owned equipment. These advances are normally amortized monthly over a period of one to five years, or even longer. This type of loan may be needed by the borrower to increase working capital, discount accounts payable, or simply to purchase new equipment. Very often an equipment loan is accepted in conjunction with accounts receivable or factoring arrangements.

Industrial time sales financing is the process of a company buying equipment from an equipment supplier and the equipment supplier selling the purchase contract to a financier.

The price you pay for buying equipment on installment is usually high; higher, in fact, than the highest interest allowable in your state. How can the additional cost of financing be higher than the maximum allowable interest rate? Because you don't pay interest on industrial installment loans—you pay a "time price differential."

The cost of buying on installment, called the "time price differential," has the following rationale: A seller is presumed to have two prices. One is the cash price; the other is the "time price," which assumes that the purchaser, who wants credit over a period of time, must pay an added charge to compensate the seller for his additional burden. The differential between the cash price and the time is the time price differential. This reasoning assumes that the seller is not a moneylender. The price doctrine provides the legal mechanism to remove the time sale from the application of usury laws (the state laws that restrict the maximum interest that can be charged on secured loans) by holding that the transaction is a credit sale and is neither a loan nor a forebearance for money.

Accounts Receivable Loans. These are the "bread and butter" of commercial finance companies, and were originally what commercial finance companies were set up to deal with. Accounts receivable loans fall into two categories: accounts receivable financing and factoring.

Accounts receivable financing at banks is practically identical to accounts receivable financing by commercial finance companies.

Accounts receivable can be pledged as collateral for loans. Typically, an 80% advance is made against eligible accounts. The assignment is handled on a nonnotification, revolving basis and is self-liquidating. Interest charges are billed on the basis of actual daily cash loan balances. This monthly charge is frequently less than missed cash discounts.

Leasing. This is a way of financing the full amount of the equipment you need. Leasing is the baby of the traditional, popular, funding methods, and there is still a lot of debate about whether it is a good method for businessmen. Furthermore, there is no standard way things can be leased. You can rent a piece of equipment with or without maintenance, or with partial maintenance, and you can lease by the month, year, or several years. You can also obtain leases with the option to purchase. The following are some advantages and disadvantages of leasing.

Advantages

1. Leasing offers a tax advantage. When you own something, you have to depreciate it for tax purposes over a lengthy period, so that the cost is recovered slowly. A lot of bookkeeping has to be done to obtain a tax saving. If inflation proceeds at the same pace as it has in recent years, the tax saving becomes one of the decreasingly valuable dollars as the depreciation table stretches into the future. Despite current efforts to slow inflation, there is little reason to expect that it can be kept under control.

    Leasing expenses are operating expenses and do not have to be depreciated, stretched out, held to future years, or back-charged to years gone by.
2. If you choose to have a maintenance contract with the lease (a good example is maintenance-included leases on copy machines), your maintenance is done by the company, and is therefore one less thing for you to worry about.
3. You can "walk away" from the lease, return the equipment to the lessor when the equipment becomes outmoded or too slow, without having to finish the payments. In short, leasing is more flexible than ownership.
4. You need not worry about the equipment becoming obsolete, because if the lease is cancelable, you just stop the lease.
5. The cost of the equipment is fixed by the lease agreement, and this makes the cost predictable for projections.
6. Money that might be tied up in expensive fixed assets can be used for other purposes.

Disadvantages

1. Down payments from leasing were at one time cheaper than purchase down payments. Now, however, the prepayment on leases is only 2 to 5% less than the down payment required for a purchase contract.
2. The costs for purchasing or buying are about the same, and when the equipment is purchased from the leasing company at the end of the period, the costs of leasing are higher.
3. If your company loses control over maintenance, you are at the mercy of the leasing company as to when the equipment will be fixed and how long the down time is.

In short, leasing requires somewhat less down payment at the start, but is generally more expensive than standard equipment purchase. Leasing is best if you need the flexibility of temporary use of the equipment.

Life Insurance Companies. Because of the striking growth of the industry, the accumulation of assets in life insurance companies has been rapid and substantial. It has been estimated that these companies are accumulating assets at the rate of $6 billion per year. The outflow of their funds can be statistically predicted. Hence, a part of their portfolio is available for long-term financing in the form of mortgages on industrial, commercial, and housing real estate. They also make loans to businesses, but require substantial enterprises with long earnings records dealing in markets not subject to rapid change. The average small or medium-sized business would not qualify because life insurance companies must follow certain loan policies: (1) the borrower has to be a corporation, (2) there is a minimum time for the borrower to be in business, and (3) the borrower should have sufficient historical and current earnings to meet obligations, including debt repayments. A life insurance company grants two types of loans: commercial and industrial mortgage loans, and unsecured loans. Mortgages by insurance companies cost the same as more orthodox bank loans.

A prevalent type of life insurance company loan is on an unsecured basis to a business in very good financial condition. Life insurance lenders are most interested in long-range financial data demonstrated by projected sales, cash flows, and so on.

Other Loan Sources.   Besides the sources mentioned above, there are other, less known sources of capital. These include credit unions, pension funds, and foundations.

Credit unions.   If you are a member of a credit union, you can receive reasonable interest loans for small amounts. Credit union services are offered only to members of credit unions; the credit union law restricts membership in a single credit union to a more or less homogeneous group of members having a common bond of interest. Credit union laws restrict the rate of interest charged and the amount of loan that may be made to a single borrower.

Pension Funds and Foundations.   Because of their regular inflow of pension money, such funds have experienced a rapid and large accumulation of assets and have a predictable outflow. Their standards of investment are similar to those of the life insurance companies, and they charge about the same interest rates.

A good percentage of pension fund money is used for sale-leasehold arrangements. Large foundations make loans in excess of $1 million for periods averaging 10 years. When they evaluate applicants, foundations place special emphasis on company management, business background, and realistic projections.

Government Loans

Guidelines for government loans differ with each organization that can grant loans, but generally the government tries to help a business to increase employment when it would otherwise be difficult for the business to do so. The government guarantees loans to businesses in financial situations that banks and other financial institutions can not or will not consider. Private and commercial lenders may not make loans if they are too large, too risky, or do not fall into the traditional lending categories.

Government loans are not easy to obtain, but sometimes government agencies loan money to extremely high risk businesses, and usually at low interest rates. However, the loan requirements are generally quite complicated.

Applying for government loans requires considerable effort, and a great deal of time must be devoted to preparing the necessary documentation. The technical requirements—that is, the proposal (analysis of your business, including budgets)—require much detail and technical work. A firm that decides to apply for government loans is advised to consult a specialist in this field. Another alternative is to read *Business Loans: A Guide to Money Sources and How to Approach Them Successfully,* by one of the authors of this book, Rick Stephan Hayes.* This book covers all the procedures and requirements of government loans in detail.

ACCOUNTING IMPLICATION OF DEBT

When a lender loans money to a business, the immediate entry is a credit to a note payable account, with an explanation of the terms and length of the loan. The following is an example for a $25,000 loan:

General journal

Date	Comment	Debit	Credit
4/7/79	Cash	$25,000	
	Long-term notes payable—Bank Amerigold		$25,000
	To record 11%, 36 month notes		
	from Bank Amerigold, payments		
	are $818.47 per month.		

An entry is then made in the general ledger as follows:

Bank Amerigold long-term
Note payable

Date	Comment	Debit	Date	Comment	Credit
			4/7/79	General Journal	$25,000

Cash

Date	Comment	Debit	Date	Comment	Credit
4/7/79	General journal	$25,000			

Whenever a payment is made to Bank Amerigold, as in the illustration above, a portion of that payment will be interest, and a portion will be principal. Interest is the amount of money that the lender charges you for using the loan. Principal is that amount of the loan repayment that is applied toward reducing the balance owed the bank. Interest is an expense and should be posted in an expense account. Principal is a reduction of the debt and is posted directly as a debit (a reduction in the amount owed) to the long-term note payable account. Interest is an expense; principal is a reduction of a liability.

Each month the lender notifies the borrower how much of the monthly payment is interest and how much is principal.

*Published by CBI of Boston, 1977.

Using as our monthly payment $818.47, with 11% interest and the total amount of the loan as $25,000 as in the example above, we get the following monthly transactions:

General journal

Date	Comment	Debit	Credit
2/20/80	Interest expense	$229.17	
	Long-term note payable	$589.30	
	Cash		$818.47
	To record monthly payment of note to Bank Amerigold (#12-34789-6)		

Ledgers

Date	Comment	Debit	Date	Comment	Credit

Interest expense

Date	Comment	Debit	Date	Comment	Credit
2/20/80	General journal	$229.17			

Bank Amerigold long-term note payable

Date	Comment	Debit	Date	Comment	Credit
			1/1/80	General journal	$25,000
2/20/80	General journal	$589.30			

Cash—Bank Amerigold

Date	Comment	Debit	Date	Comment	Credit
			2/20/80	General journal	$818.47

The interest expense can be charged off against income tax in the year of entry (1980 in the example). Principal payments are not an expense that can be charged off, but are a reduction in the balance owed on the loan. After so many payments (36 in this example), the note is paid off and the liability is reduced to zero.

When the firm designs a profit and loss statement and/or a balance sheet for banks, stockholders, government agencies, or other interested parties, a footnote should be included with these financial statements indicating the term and interest amount of the loan and the name of the asset secured by the note, if any.

"Next week," the instructor concluded, "we will talk about forms of business organization: sole proprietorship, partnership, and corporation. We'll talk about the implications of each form.

"We will also talk about owners' equity. That's the amount of money that the owners have in the business—the net worth of the business. A client once asked me what 'net worth' meant. I answered, 'To determine net worth, you take everything you have at the price you paid for it (assets), subtract what you owe on it (liabilities), and that's net worth.'

"The guy still looked mystified so I said, 'Let me give you an example: You buy a car for $10,000—that's what you paid for it—that's the asset value. You borrow $6000 from the bank to buy the car—that's the liability. The difference in what you paid—$10,000—and what you still owe—$6000—is the net worth: or $4,000.'

" 'Ohhhhhh,' he said, 'the net worth is the amount I *don't owe* any more.' " The teacher threw everything into his cardboard box. "Next week, net worth."

Chapter Seven
Forms of Business Organization

W.T. Technologies was a partnership. Lazarus Time and Ignatz Culver Whiz each owned 50% of the company. Laz had many times considered the possibility of incorporating. But all he knew about incorporating was that it limited your liability as a company and it cost at least $700 to do the legal work.

Especially now that W.T. was on the verge of getting a loan, Laz thought it might be a good idea to incorporate and limit their liability. But he wasn't too sure that the bank would like that.

Laz had questions: What are the advantages of a corporation, a partnership, or a sole proprietorship? What is stock and what does it mean? What kind of stock can a corporation have? What are the tax advantages and disadvantages of each type of organization?

Laz and Ignatz were almost finished with bringing the books up to date. They set up a meeting with Pete Popstein, their CPA. Since Pete was so busy this time of year, the appointment had to be set up for a week and a half away. Laz knew that everything could be finished by then.

At the university extension class that night there were only three people. People usually came in late, but this was the smallest class yet.

The instructor blew his nose as a starting signal and began . . .

"The principal forms of business organizations prevalent in the United States are: (1) sole proprietorships, (2) partnerships, and (3) corporations. There are also hybrid forms such as trusts, joint ventures, Subchapter-S corporations, and limited partnerships."

SOLE PROPRIETORSHIP

A sole proprietorship is the most basic form of business organization. In essence, you and your business are indistinguishable for legal, accounting, and tax purposes. Your personal assets and your business assets are in effect co-mingled, and your business income and nonbusiness income are reported to the Internal Revenue Service on the same tax form, Form 1040. Business income is simply segregated on Schedule C of Form 1040 (see Figure 7.1). About the only thing you need as a sole proprietor is a license to do business in the particular locality in which you choose to operate.

Assuming that your sole proprietorship is a bona fide business, at which you are attempting to make a living, there are certain tax advantages of this business form. First, legitimate business expenses are deductible.

This includes depreciation on property used in the business; necessary operating expenses, such as heat, light, power, telephone; reasonable travel and entertainment;

SCHEDULE C
(Form 1040)
Department of the Treasury
Internal Revenue Service

Profit or (Loss) From Business or Profession

(Sole Proprietorship)

Partnerships, Joint Ventures, etc., Must File Form 1065.

▶ Attach to Form 1040.   ▶ See Instructions for Schedule C (Form 1040).

1978

Name of proprietor	Social security number of proprietor

A Main business activity (see Instructions) ▶..; product ▶................................

B Business name ▶..

C Employer identification number ▶...

D Business address (number and street) ▶..

City, State and ZIP code ▶...

E Accounting method: **(1)** ☐ Cash   **(2)** ☐ Accrual   **(3)** ☐ Other (specify) ▶..

F Method(s) used to value closing inventory:

(1) ☐ Cost   **(2)** ☐ Lower of cost or market   **(3)** ☐ Other (if other, attach explanation)

	Yes	No

G Was there any major change in determining quantities, costs, or valuations between opening and closing inventory? . . If "Yes," attach explanation.

H Does this business activity involve oil or gas, movies or video tapes, or leasing personal (section 1245) property to others? (See page 25 of the Instructions.) . . . .

I Did you deduct expenses for an office in your home? . . . .

Part I   Income

1 a Gross receipts or sales	**1a**	
b Returns and allowances	**1b**	
c Balance (subtract line 1b from line 1a)	**1c**	
2 Cost of goods sold and/or operations (Schedule C–1, line 8)	**2**	
3 Gross profit (subtract line 2 from line 1c)	**3**	
4 Other income (attach schedule)	**4**	
5 Total income (add lines 3 and 4) . . . . ▶	**5**	

Part II   Deductions

6 Advertising			**28** Telephone		
7 Amortization			**29** Travel and entertainment . . .		
8 Bad debts from sales or services .			**30** Utilities		
9 Bank charges			**31 a** Wages . . .		
10 Car and truck expenses			**b** New Jobs Credit .		
11 Commissions			**c** Subtract line 31b from 31a .		
12 Depletion			**32** Other expenses (specify):		
13 Depreciation (explain in Schedule C–2)			**a**		
14 Dues and publications			**b**		
15 Employee benefit programs . . .			**c**		
16 Freight (not included on Schedule C–1)			**d**		
			e		
17 Insurance			**f**		
18 Interest on business indebtedness .			**g**		
19 Laundry and cleaning			**h**		
20 Legal and professional services .			**i**		
21 Office supplies			**j**		
22 Pension and profit-sharing plans .			**k**		
23 Postage			**l**		
24 Rent on business property . . .			**m**		
25 Repairs			**n**		
26 Supplies (not included on Schedule C–1)			**o**		
			p		
			q		
27 Taxes			**r**		

33 Total deductions (add amounts in columns for lines 6 through 32r) . . . . ▶   **33**

34 Net profit or (loss) (subtract line 33 from line 5). Enter here and on Form 1040, line 13. **ALSO** enter on Schedule SE (Form 1040), line 5a. (For "at risk" provisions, see page 25 of Instructions.) . . . ▶   **34**

Figure 7.1

SCHEDULE C–1.—Cost of Goods Sold and/or Operations (See Schedule C Instructions for Part I, Line 2)

1 Inventory at beginning of year (if different from last year's closing inventory, attach explanation) .	1	
2 a Purchases	2a	
b Cost of items withdrawn for personal use	2b	
c Balance (subtract line 2b from line 2a)	2c	
3 Cost of labor (do not include salary paid to yourself)	3	
4 Materials and supplies	4	
5 Other costs (attach schedule)	5	
6 Add lines 1, 2c, and 3 through 5	6	
7 Inventory at end of year	7	
8 **Cost of goods sold and/or operations** (subtract line 7 from line 6). Enter here and on Part I, line 2 . ▶	8	

SCHEDULE C–2.—Depreciation (See Schedule C Instructions for line 13)
If you need more space, please use Form 4562.

Description of property (a)	Date acquired (b)	Cost or other basis (c)	Depreciation allowed or allowable in prior years (d)	Method of computing depreciation (e)	Life or rate (f)	Depreciation for this year (g)
1 Total additional first-year depreciation (do not include in items below) ⟶						
2 Other depreciation:						
Buildings						
Furniture and fixtures						
Transportation equipment . .						
Machinery and other equipment .						
Other (Specify) _____						
3 Totals					3	
4 Depreciation claimed in Schedule C–1					4	
5 Balance (subtract line 4 from line 3). Enter here and on Part II, line 13 . . . . ▶					5	

SCHEDULE C–3.—Expense Account Information (See Schedule C Instructions for Schedule C–3)

Enter information for yourself and your five highest paid employees. In determining the five highest paid employees, add expense account allowances to the salaries and wages. However, you don't have to provide the information for any employee for whom the combined amount is less than $25,000, or for yourself if your expense account allowance plus line 34, page 1, is less than $25,000.

Name (a)	Expense account (b)	Salaries and Wages (c)
Owner		
1 _____		
2 _____		
3 _____		
4 _____		
5		

Did you claim a deduction for expenses connected with:	Yes	No
A Entertainment facility (boat, resort, ranch, etc.)?		
B Living accommodations (except employees on business)?		
C Employees' families at conventions or meetings?		
If "Yes," were any of these conventions or meetings outside the U.S. or its possessions? (See page 26 of Instructions.) .		
D Vacations for employees or their families not reported on Form W–2?		

☆ U.S. GOVERNMENT PRINTING OFFICE : 1978—O–263-056　94-0743750

Figure 7.1 *(Continued)*

and so on. If your business is conducted out of your home, the portion of your home that is devoted to business will be considered property used in the business. Salaries and wages paid to employees of your business are deductible expenses. Furthermore, legitimate pension, profit sharing, and hospital and accident insurance deductions may be available.

PARTNERSHIP

A partnership may be nothing more than two or more sole proprietors who have agreed to pool their assets and operate a business jointly. There does not have to be a formal agreement between the partners in order for a partnership to exist legally, or for tax purposes. However, most states have partnership laws, and written partnership agreements should be drawn up by a lawyer in conformity with the laws of your particular state. For federal income tax purposes, the word partnership applies not only to a partnership as it is known in common law, but also a syndicate, group, pool, joint venture, or other unincorporated organization which carries on any business and which is not defined as a trust, an estate, or a corporation.

A partnership is not taxable as such. Only the members of the partnership are taxed in their individual capacities on their share of the partnership taxable income, whether distributed to them or not.

Example. A partnership is composed of two partners sharing profits equally. In the current year, the taxable income of the business is $30,000, none of which is distributed to the partners. The partnership tax return will report the $30,000 and show shares of $15,000 to each of the partners. Each partner will report his share of the partnership taxable income on his own tax return, even though the income has not been distributed to him.

The character of the income earned by a partnership is not altered when the income passes to the partners. For example, if a partnership sells a building and realizes a long-term capital gain on the transaction, the long-term capital gain is passed through to the partners rather than being reflected as part of the partnership income. The types of income, losses, and expenses which are passed to partners include ordinary income and loss, additional first year depreciation, dividends, interest, short-term capital gains, long-term capital gains, and contributions.

Partnership Accounting

If your company is a partnership, separate capital and drawing accounts must be kept for each partner. If no other agreement has been made, the law provides that all partnership earnings are to be shared equally; but the partners may agree in advance to any method of sharing earnings. If they have losses, losses are shared in the same way as earnings.

At the end of every year, your company's profits (or losses) must be distributed to each partner's capital account. Partners, like sole proprietors, cannot actually receive salaries from their company. A partner works for partnership profits. You may, however, wish to allocate the equivalent of "salaries" or "interest" payments, or both, to partners as a way of compensating each one fairly for time and capital invested in the business.

Limited Partnership

A limited partnership is a special type of partnership authorized under many state laws. A limited partnership must have at least one general partner, who has unlimited liability for the debts of the partnership, and who is responsible for managing the business. The limited partners are only liable to the extent of their partnership interests, and they must not participate in any way in the management of the business. The advantage of a limited partnership is that it may employ leverage, to earn a higher rate of return of the limited partners' invested capital than would otherwise be the case, without increasing the risk of the limited partner.

Example. A contractor becomes the general partner in a limited partnership. He agrees to acquire land, construct a building, and sell the building when it is completed. He arranges for five investors to contribute $20,000 each to the project in exchange for limited partnership interests. On the basis of the construction plans, and the $100,000 equity, the contractor-general partner is able to arrange a bank loan for $200,000. Considerable leverage would be used, and most of the money contributed by the limited partners, and even that which was borrowed, would be treated as a tax deductible expense in the year of the formation of the partnership.

In an attempt to discourage the proliferation of tax shelters Congress passed the Tax Reform Act of 1976, which curtailed tax shelters. Basically, the rule became one where the amount of losses that could be claimed from certain investment activities could not exceed the total amount that the taxpayer had at risk in the partnership. Under the "at risk" rule, loss deductions are limited to the amount of cash contributed to the partnership by the partner. There is no liability for the limited partners beyond their initial investment. When a building is sold, the limited partners will share in the profits.

A great many tax shelters are constructed as limited partnerships because of the leverage advantages (see Figure 7.2).

SUB-CHAPTER S CORPORATIONS

In the eyes of the law, a corporation is a person, and it can sue, be sued, and also pay taxes. Since the individuals who own the corporation also pay taxes on any dividends they receive from the corporation, there is in effect double taxation.

Many people argue that this double taxation should be eliminated. To a certain extent the double taxation has been eliminated by the creation of Small Business Corporations, also referred to as tax option corporations, or Sub-Chapter S corporations.

A Sub-Chapter S corporation is a corporation that has elected, by unanimous consent of its shareholders, not to pay any corporate tax on its income. Instead, the

	Limited Partner	General Partner
Management project	No	Yes
Liability for project debt	No	Yes
Equity investment	Yes	No
Investment tax-deductable	Yes	No

Figure 7.2

shareholders pay taxes on it, even though it is not distributed. Shareholders of a Sub-Chapter S corporation are entitled to deduct, on their individual returns, their share of any net operating loss sustained by the corporations.

Unlike a partnership, a Sub-Chapter S corporation is not a conduit. That is, individual items of income and deduction are not passed through to the shareholders to retain the same character in the hands of those shareholders as they had in the hands of the corporation. Instead, taxable income is computed at the corporate level in much the same way as it is computed for any other corporation. The shareholders are then taxed directly on this taxable income, whether or not the corporation makes any distributions to them. There is one exception to this no conduit rule. The Sub-Chapter S corporation's net capital gains or losses are passed to shareholders and are treated by them as long-term capital gains or losses on their individual returns.

Only a domestic corporation that is not a member of an affiliated group can elect Sub-Chapter S status. A qualifying Sub-Chapter S corporation may have no more than one class of stock and no more than 10 shareholders. The shareholders must all be individuals, or estates of deceased individuals, who were shareholders. Beginning in 1977, the number of shareholders in a Sub-Chapter S corporation may be increased to 15 if and only if the Sub-Chapter S corporation has been in existence for five years.

The tax aspects of a Sub-Chapter S corporation are somewhat complex. A certified public accountant should be consulted if you decide that Sub-Chapter S status is an appropriate form of business organization for your particular business.

CORPORATIONS

Most businesses that are not designed strictly for investment purposes eventually decide to incorporate. Their reasons include: limits on personal liability of owner-managers, financing and growth flexibility, and transferability of interest.

The first decision faced by persons who would like to incorporate a business is where to incorporate. A corporation depends on legal statutes of a particular state for its permission to exist. Some state corporation laws are more attractive to incorporators than others. Some states have attracted incorporation far out of proportion to the number of corporations actually doing business there. For example, Delaware has had, for many years, a corporation law that offers incorporators certain privileges, advantages, and facilities for incorporation that could not be obtained elsewhere.

Recently, however, differences in corporation laws among the major commercial states have been reduced, and businesses often prefer to incorporate in the state where the major share of the business will be done.

Although the procedure of incorporation varies in detail from state to state, the pattern is much the same everywhere. Certain steps should be taken before the incorporators draw up a charter. Included among these are: the discovery and investigation of a business opportunity, developing financial and promotional arrangements, arranging for property and material supply, solicitation of preincorporation stock subscriptions, and reservation of a corporate name.

Corporate Charters

Corporate charters are required to have certain clauses, and are permitted to have others (see Figure 7.3). Usually the first clause of a corporate charter is the corporate name. The name cannot conflict with any other name used in that state. Names of individual incorporators should not be used because of the potential danger that they might lose the right to use their own names for business purposes.

Charter

Corporate name
Business purpose
Capital structure
Location of principal offered
Number of shares
Number of directors
Names and addresses of directors
Existence of preemptive rights
Specific and collective rights
Others

Bylaws

Duties and compensation of corporate officers
Qualification of membership on board of directors
Director committees
Date and place of annual stockholder meeting
Provision for audits
Others

Figure 7.3   Corporate charter.

A second clause will contain the business purpose. This sets forth the purposes, objects, or general nature of the business. Many states permit a purpose clause to include a general statement that the corporation is formed for any lawful purpose.

Most corporation laws require a third clause of the corporate charter to outline the proposed corporation's capital structure, including the authorized number of shares, the rights, preferences, privileges and restrictions on the various classes and series of shares, whether the shares have a par value, and the voting rights of the shares.

Other provisions appearing in the charter pertain to the location of the principal office, the number of directors, the names and addresses of the original directors, the duration of the corporation, the existence of preemptive rights, the powers of directors, a statement that the corporation may become a partner in a partnership, and other provisions.

The bylaws of a corporation deal with the internal management rules of the corporation. They must be consistent with the charter of the corporation. Bylaws usually deal with matters such as the duties and compensation of corporation officers, the qualifications for membership on the board of directors, executive and other director committees, the date and place of annual shareholders meetings, provisions for audits, and other matters (see Figure 7.3).

The financing of a corporation is accomplished primarily through two means: debt and equity. Debt financing is discussed in Chapter 6, Liabilities.

Equity financing of a corporation is obtained through issuance of common stock or preferred stock.

The rights of the holders of common stock in a business corporation are established by the laws of the state in which the corporation is chartered and by the terms of the charters. The terms of charters are relatively uniform on many matters, some of which have been described previously.

In addition, the following two matters are usually addressed in corporate charters with respect to rights of common stockholders.

Collective Rights.   Certain collective rights are usually given to the holders of common stock. Some of the more important rights allow stockholders to amend the charter, to adopt bylaws, to elect directors, to authorize sale of major assets, to enter into mergers, to change the amount of authorized common stock, and to issue preferred stock, debentures, bonds, and other securities.

Specific Rights.   Holders of common stock also have specific rights, as do individual owners. They have the right to vote. They may sell their ownership shares. They have the right to inspect the corporate books.

Advantages and Disadvantages of Common Stock Financing

There are four principal advantages of using common stock as a source of financing for a corporation:

1. Common stock does not entail fixed charges. As the company generates the earnings, it can pay common stock dividends. In contrast to bond interest, there is no legal obligation to pay dividends.
2. Common stock carries no fixed maturity date.
3. Since common stock provides a cushion against losses for creditors, the sale of common stock increases the credit worthiness of the firm.
4. Common stock may at times be sold more easily than debt. This is true because common stock may have a higher expected return in a period of inflation and the return will increase, whereas the return on debt remains constant.

There are several disadvantages of using common stock as a source of financing for a corporation:

1. The sale of common stock extends voting rights or control to the additional stockholders. For this reason, additional equity financing is often avoided by small and new firms. The owner-managers may be unwilling to share control of their companies with outsiders.
2. Common stock gives more owners the right to share in profits. The use of debt may enable the company to employ funds at a fixed low cost, whereas common stock gives equal rights to new stockholders to share in the net profits of the company.
3. The costs of underwriting and distributing common stock are usually higher than for underwriting and distributing preferred stock or debt. Underwriting costs for selling common stock are higher because the costs of investigating an equity security investment are greater than for a comparable debt security. Also, common stocks are more risky, which means equity holdings must be diversified. This means that a given dollar amount of new stock must be sold to a greater number of purchasers than the same amount of debt.
4. Common stock dividends are not deductible for tax purposes, but bond interest is.

Par and No Par Stock.   Common stock either has a par value assigned to it by the issuing company, or it is no par stock. Par value is an arbitrary amount assigned to a share of stock and has no necessary relationship to its market value at any given time. For accounting purposes, no par stock is assigned a stated value per share by the issuing company, and this is the basis on which the stock is presented in the balance sheet.

The excess price above either the par or stated value received at the time stock is sold initially is entered in an account entitled "paid-in surplus," "capital surplus," or "capital in excess of par or stated value," the balance of which on the balance sheet appears as a separate item in the capital section of that statement (see Figure 7.4).

Assume 9500 shares sold at $5 per share

Yourcompany Stockholder's Equity

Common stock, $1 par value (Authorized: 10,000 shares issued and outstanding: 9500)	$ 9,500
Capital in excess of par value	38,000
Total stockholder's equity	$47,500

Figure 7.4   Stockholder's equity section of balance sheet.

Preferred Stock

Preferred stock has claims or rights ahead of common stock, but behind those of debt securities. The preference may be a prior claim on earnings, it may take the form of a prior claim on assets in the event of liquidation, or it may take a preferential position with regard to both earnings and assets. The hybrid nature of preferred stock becomes apparent when one tries to classify it in relation to debt securities and common stocks. The priority feature and the fixed dividend indicate that preferred stock is similar to debt. Payments to preferred stockholders are limited in amount, so that common stockholders receive the advantages or disadvantages of leverage. However, if the preferred dividends are not earned, the company can forgo paying them without damage of bankruptcy. In this way, preferred stock is similar to common stock.

The possible characteristics, rights, and obligations vary widely. As economic conditions change, new types of securities are invented. The possibilities are many, limited only by the imagination and ingenuity of the managers formulating the terms of the security issues. It is not surprising, then, that preferred stock can be found in a variety of forms. Some of the more common features of preferred stock are:

- Preference in assets and earning.
- Par or liquidation value (dividends as a percentage of par).
- Cumulative dividends (i.e. all dividends in arrears must be paid).
- Convertibility into common stock.
- Participation in earnings.
- Call provision.

Comparison.   A comparison of the different types of business—sole proprietorship, partnership, corporation, and Sub-Chapter S corporation appears in Figure 7.5.

	Sole Proprietorship	Partnership	Sub-Chapter S Corporation	Corporation
Net profit of company taxed as owner's individual income	Yes	Yes	Yes	No
Owners have legal liability	Yes	Yes	No	No
Company has legal liability	No	No	Yes	Yes
Company tax deductions passed to owners (conduit transaction)	Yes	Yes	No	No
Corporate division of an affiliated group			No	Yes
Company has more than one class of voting stock			No	Yes
Company has more than 10 to 15 stockholders			No	Yes
Stock can be held by other corporations			No	Yes

Figure 7.5   Comparison of business types.

TRANSFORMING THE STRUCTURE OF A BUSINESS

One of the few remaining ways to become a well-to-do person in the United States is to start a business enterprise, make it a success, take the company public in a stock offering (retaining a healthy share of the stock yourself), and then see the stock rise significantly in price in the public market. This, of course, is a long shot gamble; but if you win. . . .

Some lawyers, accountants and investment bankers make a specialty of taking new companies into the public markets. Their goal is to be part of the long shot when it comes through. The tax implications of moving away from proprietorship and partnership towards a corporation are such that generally accepted accounting principles (such as concepts of accrual, depreciation, inventory, etc.) are more frequently brought into play in corporations. The business manager in a corporate setting has to be more aware of his accounting options, and the business's accountant has to be more aware of generally accepted standards of accounting and auditing, and not just of taxes.

When a corporation decides to go into a public issue of stock, it may want to do many things from an accounting standpoint. For example, in a private company, saving taxes may be paramount; whereas in a public company, saving taxes is important, but reported earnings may be equally important. Therefore, a company moving from private to public status may want to reassess its depreciation and amortization policy along with other accounting treatments, such as bad debt allowances, warranty reserves, inventory valuation, and so forth.

Going public may mean that your company will be audited for the first time by a certified public accountant. Many local CPAs are highly competent at tax returns and tax planning, and at preparing financial reports from client records, but are only rarely engaged to perform certified audits. It is generally not possible for a CPA who is closely allied as an advisor to your business and preparer of financial statements, to perform a certified audit. Going public often means you have to find a new CPA firm. This can be a costly and somewhat traumatic process. The chief benefit is that you obtain a thorough review of your business from an objective standpoint, and an assurance that your financial statements are prepared in conformity with generally accepted accounting principles. Such conformity, plus a unqualified opinion from a respected CPA firm, will enhance the marketability of the stock of your company. This means more money if your stock is sold successfully.

A public issue of stock requires several outside consultants—notably an accountant and a lawyer with prior experience in public securities offerings, and a securities underwriter or investment banker. Each of these persons will have a role to play in the issuing of public securities. The accountant must prepare a certified audit opinion upon completion of his audit of your business. The lawyer will typically prepare the written parts of any forms and documents that must be filed with the securities or franchise board of the state of incorporation or with the Securities and Exchange Commission (SEC).

Typically, no documents will be required if the total funds raised are less than $100,000. If the total funds raised are between $100,000 and $500,000, you may be able to avoid filing many of these documents by complying with Regulation A of the Securities Act of 1933, which specifies an exemption for small offerings. If the total funds raised are over $500,000, it will probably be necessary to undergo a complete registration statement procedure. The registration statement will be filed with, and reviewed by the SEC in Washington, D.C., or a regional field office.

Upon completion of the review, the registration is said to "go effective" and your stock may be legally sold in the public markets. This is where the underwriter plays a role in the issuance and sale. His job is to judge the movement of the market and to estimate the best time to begin selling the stock in the public market. The underwriter typically receives as a fee a certain percentage of the total amount raised, or, as an alterantive, will purchase the new stock at a price which is estimated to be below the market price when the stock is sold publicly. In the latter case, the risk of stock price decline is often on the underwriter—hence the name "underwriter."

Most companies that are initially required to file registration statements in conjunction with sales of stock will be compelled to file additional annual, quarterly, and other update reports and to revise their registration statements, prospectuses and proxy materials from time to time. This is an added cost in terms of the time involved for management, accountant's and lawyer's fees, and probable printing costs. Such costs should be considered when initially planning a public issue of stock or other securities.

"That's it. I've got to leave early tonight. I'll just take some questions," the instructor said.

Lazarus asked the question for which he had waited an hour. "You told us last time about loans, this time about types of businesses: sole proprietorship, partnership, and corporation. My company is a partnership now. We are contemplating a loan. Would it help our legal liability on that loan if we were a corporation?"

The instructor paused to think for a moment. Lazarus wondered if he had stumped the teacher. The pause lasted a little longer. Finally, when everyone was about to give up, the instructor replied, "No. Even if you are a corporation the bank can still ask for personal guarantees of the owners. The only time the corporate umbrella would really protect you as an owner would be if your company were large enough to go public. In the cases of smaller corporations, the banks generally require personal guarantees of the owners."

The instructor paused. There were no more questions, so he said "Goodbye."

As the class was leaving Lazarus noticed a man in a chauffeur's uniform waiting in front of the building. Lazarus paused a while in the parking lot to see whom the chauffeur was waiting for. He saw the chauffeur jump and start moving toward the street. Lazarus could just barely make out the face of the person who was leaving the building. It was the teacher, the instructor of his class.

Chapter Eight
Revenue and Expense

"What can we write off?" This was the first question that Lazarus Time and Ignatz Culver Whiz discussed when they started W.T. Technologies. The second thing they talked about was "What's business income and what's personal income?"

It was obvious that Ignatz needed the use of a car for the business. He had been using his old Ford Falcon wagon and it was about to break down. How much of the present car and the one they wanted to buy could be written off as a business expense? How about gasoline and repairs? When Ignatz filled the tank, who was paying for it—him or the business? When Laz traveled on business, just what part of the trip was a business expense?

Everyone was glad to tell Laz what business expenses were and how much of what he would write off. Unfortunately, everyone gave him a different opinion. And some of the stuff some of the people told him he could write off he *knew* he couldn't. Everyone had advice, but all the advice was different, and some of it was just plain wrong.

Lazarus had to worry about two types of business income—the income of W.T. Technologies and the income he received as a consultant to W.T.

W.T. Technologies had income from the sale of holographic memory machines, related supplies, and related repair services. How were these incomes treated?

Laz was running late that night and the instructor had already begun.

"In this lecture we will discuss revenues, or sales, and expenses. Revenues and expenses are important to every business. No business can operate without expenses, and no business will operate very long without revenues or sales. . . ."

REVENUE (SALES OR INCOME)

To a salesman, a sale takes place when he receives an order from a customer, but to the accountant it is not a sale until the goods are shipped. A statistical record or order is kept for management purposes, but a sale is not a sale until the goods are out the door. When goods have been shipped, the accountant will accept the fact that delivery has been made, and, accordingly, records the event as a sale.

Thus, for the majority of companies, the word "sales" in an income statement means goods shipped during a given accounting period.

To a business consultant, however, sales means fees for services performed as well as other items of income such as commissions, rents, and royalties.

For sales involving the shipment of goods, there is normally a passing of legal title, which is evidence that a sale has in fact taken place. In service business transactions however, revenue recognition is not dependent on the passing of title. A business consultant does not pass a legal title when he or she performs a service for a client.

Taxable Income

According to the tax code, gross income includes but is not limited to:

1. Income from trade or business
2. Compensation for services, including fees, commissions and similar items
3. Gains derived from dealings in property
4. Interest income
5. Dividends
6. Rents
7. Royalties
8. Income from the discharge of indebtedness
9. Distributive share of partnership gross income

Income is created whenever there is a billing of fees for services rendered. In other words, when the client is billed, the amount billed is considered to be income.

Besides the above, other items of income include bond premiums, capital gains from the sale of assets, property received for services performed, promissory notes, recovery of damages, and recovery of items previously deducted for income tax purposes.

Recovery of damages received as a result of patent infringement and breach of contract, or of a fiduciary duty, are included in gross income when they are received. Ordinary damages are not taxable, but punitive damages are.

Property received in lieu of cash is considered business income. Any material you receive in lieu of cash payment for fees is considered income and is valued at the fair market of the item at the time it is received.

Exchange of property for like property is not considered to be income. Like property means physical property that is similar in type. An exchange of real estate for real estate is a like property exchange, as is an exchange of personal property (such as equipment) for personal property.

In any business in which inventory is not a factor in determining income, such as business consultants, gross sales (less returns and allowances) *is equivalent to* gross profit. Most professions and businesses that provide personal services determine gross profit as gross sales.

OPERATING EXPENSE

Operating expenses and selling expenses are listed in an income statement after the figure for gross margin. Both selling and operating expenses are sometimes listed simply under "operating expenses," "general and administrative expense," or just "expenses."

General and administrative expenses are costs to be deducted from gross profit to arrive at operating income. From a budgeting and control standpoint, these are managed costs and in the short run they will be fixed costs. They are regulated over time by management decisions and do not necessarily bear any direct relationship to production or sales volume.

Items Included in Operating and Selling Expense

There are certain expenses that are tax deductible and others that are not. We will group these items as follows: wages and salaries, rental expense, repairs, replacements, and improvements, travel and transportation, business entertainment, interest, insurance, taxes, and other business expense. Each of these groups will be discussed in turn.

Wages and Salaries. Salaries, wages and other forms of compensation paid to employees are deductible business expenses for tax purposes if they meet the following four tests (see Figure 8.1):

Test 1. You must be able to show that salaries, wages, and other compensation are "ordinary and necessary expenditures directly connected with carrying on [your] business or trade." The fact that you pay your employees reasonable compensation for legitimate business purposes is not enough, by itself, to qualify the expense as a deductible expense. Remunerations of services can be deducted only if the payment is an ordinary and necessary expense of carrying on your trade or business. Expenses (including salaries) incurred in completing mergers, recapitalizations, consolidations, and other reorganizations are not expenses of carrying on a business unless the reorganization, merger, or whatever, falls through. If the merger or reorganization is abandoned, the expenses of that reorganization are deducted in that year.

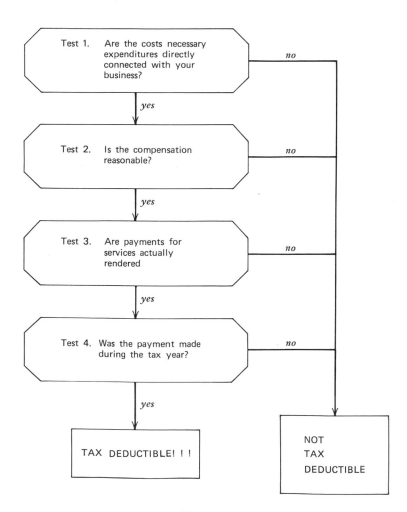

Figure 8.1

Test 2. Reasonable compensation is determined by the amount that "ordinarily would be paid for like services, by like enterprises, under like circumstances." The following factors are considered in determining reasonableness of compensation:

- Duties performed by the employee.
- Volume of business handled.
- Character and amount of responsibility.
- Complexities of the business.
- Amount of time required.
- General cost of living in the locality.
- Ability and achievements of the individual performing the service.
- Comparison of the compensation with the amount of gross and net income of the business.

As a practical matter, however, most compensation deducted never gets questioned. If the amount of compensation is questioned, the factors listed above serve as a basis for determining reasonableness.

Test 3. You must be able to prove that the payments were made for services actually rendered. You must also reasonably expect your business to benefit from the service performed.

Test 4. You must have paid the compensation or incurred the expense during the tax year. Using the cash accounting method, only salaries actually paid during the year are deductible. If you use the accrual method of accounting, the deduction for salaries and wages is allowable when the obligation to pay the compensation is established.

Bonuses you pay to employees are allowable deductions if they are intended as additional compensation, not gifts, and are paid for services actually rendered. If, to promote employee goodwill, you distribute turkeys, hams, or other merchandise of nominal value at Christmas time and on other special occasions, the value of these gifts is not considered salary or wages to your employees. You can deduct the cost of these gifts as a business expense, however, under the gift category. These gifts are limited to a $25 value per person. If, however, you distribute cash, gift certificates, or similar items of readily convertible cash value, the value of such gifts is considered additional wages or salary, regardless of amount.

Compensation need not be paid in cash. It may be in the form of meals, lodging, capital assets, or shares of stock in the business.

Fringe benefits such as premiums on insurance, hospitalization, and medical care for employees are deductible by the employer. This does not include life insurance premiums except under special circumstances (there is a $25,000 term insurance limit).

Rental Expenses. You may ordinarily deduct, as current expenses, rent paid or accrued for property used in your trade or business.

Rent paid on property is deductible as rent to the extent of the fair market value of that property or service.

Rent paid in advance, sums paid to acquire a lease, and commissions, bonuses, fees, or other expenses you pay to obtain possession of property under a lease must be deducted over the term of the lease, or the period covered by the advance.

Repairs, Replacements, and Improvements.   Expenditures for property or equipment may or may not be deductible as expenses, depending on whether they only maintain the property or actually add to the value and life of the property.

Repairs, including labor, supplies, and certain other items *are* deductible expenses, because repairs generally just maintain property. The value of your own labor expended in a repair, however, is not deductible as an expense. Examples of repairs include patching and repairing floors, repainting the inside and outside of a building, repairing roofs and gutters, and mending leaks.

Replacements that arrest deterioriation and appreciably prolong the life of the property are *not* deductible as expense. They should be capitalized and depreciated. Expenditures for replacements parts of a machine to maintain it in operable condition *are* deductible business expenses. Major overhauls of machinery require capitalization and depreciation.

Travel and Transportation Expenses.   Travel expenses are costs incurred traveling away from home overnight in pursuit of your trade or business. Transportation expenses, on the other hand, include only the costs of travel (not meals and lodging) directly attributable to the actual conduct of your business while you are *not* away from home overnight.

Travel expenses include meals and lodging (both en route and at your destination), air, rail, and bus fares, baggage charges, the cost of transporting sample cases or display materials, the cost of maintaining and operating your automobile, the cost of operating and maintaining your house trailer, reasonable cleaning and laundry expenses, telephone and telegraph expenses, and the cost of a public stenographer.

Travel expenses also include:

- The cost of transportation from the airport or station to your hotel, from your hotel to the airport or station, from one customer or place of work to another.
- Reasonable transportation costs from where you obtain meals and lodging to where you are working while away from home overnight.
- Other similar expenses incidental to qualifying travel.
- Reasonable tips incidental to any of the expenses.

You can deduct travel expenses you incur for yourself—but not for your family—in attending a convention. Incidental personal expenses incurred for your entertainment, sightseeing, social visiting, and so on, are not deductible.

Transportation expenses (sometimes referred to as local travel expenses) include such items as air, train, bus, and cab fares, and the expenses of operating and maintaining your business vehicle. Commuting expenses between your residence and usual place of business are not deductible regardless of the distance involved.

If you use your automobile entirely for business purposes, you can deduct all of your actual expenses for its operation, including depreciation. However, if your automobile is used only partly for business, you must apportion its expense and a reasonable allowance for depreciation between business and personal usage.

If you lease a car for use in your business, you can deduct your lease payments to the extent that they are directly attributable to your business. You cannot deduct any portion of the lease payments for commuting or other personal use of the car.

Instead of using actual expenses and depreciation to determine deductible costs of operating an automobile (including pick-up or panel truck) for business purposes, you can use a standard mileage rate of 17 cents a mile for the first 15,000 miles of business usage per year, and 10 cents a mile for each additional business mile in that year. To use the standard mileage rate, you must:

- Own your car.
- Not use more than one car simultaneously in your business or profession.
- Not use the car for hire, such as taxi.
- Not operate a fleet of cars of which two or more are used simultaneously.
- Not have claimed depreciation using any method other than the straight line method.
- Not have claimed additional first-year depreciation on the car.

If the car is fully depreciated you can only deduct 10 cents a mile for all miles of business usage.

Parking fees and tolls incurred during business use are deductible in addition to the standard mileage rate.

Business Entertainment Expenses. Entertainment includes any activity generally considered to be entertainment, amusement, or recreation. Usually, this covers entertaining guests at restaurants, theaters, and sporting events, and on yachts, on hunting or fishing vacations, or similar trips. Entertainment expense includes satisfying the personal or family needs of any individuals, the cost of which would be a business expense to you. Examples are furnishing food and beverages, providing a hotel suite, and providing an automobile to business customers or their families.

Items are considered business entertainment expenses and deductible only if they are ordinary and necessary expenses "directly related to or associated with the active conduct of your trade or business."

Interest Expense. Interest is defined as "the compensation allowed by law or fixed by the parties for the use (or forbearance) of money." A business can deduct all interest paid or accrued in the tax year on a business debt. The interest paid must be on a debt under which you have a valid obligation to "pay a fixed and determinable sum of money." This debt is generally referred to as a liability.

Insurance Expense. If you carry business insurance to protect your company against losses by fire or other hazards, the premiums paid are deductible as business expenses. The following are sample deductible expenses:

- Premiums on fire, theft, flood, or other casualty insurance
- Credit insurance
- Employee's group hospitalization and medical insurance
- Premiums on employer's liability insurance
- Malpractice insurance
- Public liability insurance
- Workman's compensation insurance
- Overhead insurance
- Use and occupancy insurance and business interruption
- Employee performance bonds
- Expenses for bonds the business is required to furnish either by law or by contract
- Automobile and other vehicle insurance (unless you use the standard mileage rate to compute auto expense)

Tax Expense.   Various taxes, imposed by federal, state, local, and foreign governments and incurred in the ordinary course of business or trade, are deductible. Taxes that are *not* deductible include federal income, estate, and gift taxes; state inheritance, legacy, and succession taxes; and assessments for local benefits. Assessments for local benefits are those that tend to increase the value of your property (such as assessments for construction of streets, sidewalks, public parking facilities, and water and sewage systems).

Taxes that are deductible as business expenses are broken down into broad categories:

- Real property taxes
- Income tax
- Other taxes
- Employment taxes (payroll, social security, etc.)

"That's all for tonight. I'm going to end the class early," the instructor said. "I have a very important meeting." He ran out without even taking any questions.

Laz was getting tired of this class, and of the instructor running out early—even though there weren't many people left in the class.

What Laz missed most was talking to Suzi Wo—she was real cute. And she was funny. Suzi hadn't come to the class recently. In the last couple of meetings, as a matter of fact, Laz hadn't seen her.

When Laz stepped outside the building, he was blinded by the headlights of a limousine. He could see the instructor inside, and he could see that there was someone in the back seat with him. Laz speculated about this mysterious other person.

Chapter Nine
The Financial Statements

Lazarus Time and Ignatz Whiz were sitting at Ignatz's desk when the CPA Pete Popstein came in. "So you've finished the books?" he asked.

"Yeah, here they are." Lazarus handed Pete the ledgers and journals.

"Okay," Pete thumbed through the books, "Yeah, it looks okay. . . . Now what I'm going to do today is give you guys an idea of what this posting from the books is all about. I'll tell you a little bit about the philosophy of accounting. Then I'll explain to you some of the general concepts of an income statement, balance sheet, and sources and uses of funds statements. These are the financial statements that the bank wants for the loan.

"That will be all for today. I'll take the books to the office and post the actual financial statements from your books. When I come back, I'll explain how it got from your books to the financial statements. Okay?" Pete concluded and looked at Laz and Ignatz.

"Okay," said Ignatz. "When will you come back?"

"It's hard to say, because this is the middle of the accounting season. But I'll try to do it within the next four days," Pete answered.

"Okay," said Lazarus. "I know you're busy, so let's start talking."

Pete Popstein began.

An accounting period can be a maximum of one year and usually not less than one month. Large corporations which have stock traded in the public market usually end their accounting period every three months and then obtain final totals at the end of a year. Smaller businesses like W.T. Technologies usually end their accounting period at the end of a year, and they total up what their transactions were for the year for income tax purposes.

W.T. Technologies will have a 6 month statement. At the end of a period, all of the accounts that a business has (assets, liabilities, equity, income, and expenses) have to be totaled and summarized.

The summarizing process performed on a business's books is called "closing the books." The accountant transfers all the totals of all the accounts for one year to a summary sheet.

THE ASSUMPTIONS OF ACCOUNTING FOR BUSINESS

To understand the process of closing the books you must understand the primary assumptions of accounting in regard to business. These assumptions are:

First, businesses are ongoing entities with unlimited life.

Second, although businesses have unlimited lifetimes, they require an "accounting" of their actions at least once per year.

Third, there is a part of a business's accounts that lives forever and another part that "dies" each time an accounting is made. That is, a business will have both permanent and cyclical accounts.

Every business is expected to continue until the owner sells or retires, and it is in this spirit that the accounting records are kept. A business may in fact exist on a moment-to-moment basis with an unpredictable future. But this line of thinking is not in accord with a logical system. And accounting is *above all* a logical system.

The second assumption, that businesses with an unlimited lifetime require periodic "accountings," is fairly recent. In the early days, there was really no reason to summarize the accounts at the end of a period because transactions were relatively few and simple. As the number of accounts grew, the importance of periodically summarizing the transactions became important for two reasons: (1) It provided a "milestone" to compare how the business did in the past with how it is doing now. The periodic accountings (closing of the books) of a business are the measure of the business's past performance against its present performance. (2) In most countries (including the United States), a periodic accounting is required by law.

Governments that tax their business organizations require that every business prepare a summary of its business performance (sales, expenses, profit, etc.). The businesses are then taxed on the basis of these summaries. The summaries that the United States government requires of business are called "income statements" (or profit and loss statements) and statements of financial condition (balance sheet). If the company is publicly traded it must provide annual reports and financial statements quarterly.

These "summaries" that business provides to the government are for a period no longer than one year by law.*

The third assumption, that there is a part of a business's accounts that has only a limited (cyclical) life and another part that is permanent, is a result of the periodic accounting assumption. Some account information is only needed for a one period summary.

For example, sales for last year are not needed to calculate this year's sales. Expenses and cost of sales that you incurred last year should not be added to this year's expense and cost of sales. Sales, expenses, and cost of sales records need only exist for the one period that they are used to calculate profit or loss. These are "cyclical" accounts.

Some accounts continue as the business does. The accounts are never closed, but are simply summarized and brought forward each year. These "permanent accounts" are assets, liabilities, and equity. Obviously, if you owe someone money at the end of one period (liabilities such as mortgages) that debt obligation will continue into the next period. If someone owes you money (accounts receivable—an asset), this obligation will also continue into the next year.

BUSINESS FINANCIAL STATEMENTS

Business financial statements include:

- The income statement (profit and loss statement)
- The statement of financial condition (balance sheet)
- Statement of retained earnings and funds flow statement

*There are some exceptions to this one year rule in the tax codes. An exception would be when a company can show that its business cycle requires that the period be longer (up to 13 months).

The most used of the financial statements is the income statement—the IRS requires an income statement for all businesses. The income statement is a summary of money that came into the business (revenue or income), money that was spent (cost of sales and expenses), and how much money remained after costs were paid (net profit).

The next most widely used financial statement is the balance sheet. The IRS does not require partnerships and proprietorships to file a balance sheet with their income tax returns. Because they are not required, many businesses do not understand or use them. The balance sheet is a summary of what the business owns (assets), what it owes (liabilities), and how much of the owner's money is in the business (equity).

To explain the difference between a balance sheet and an income statement, the analogy of a moving train is often used.

Let's assume that there are two photographers assigned to document the last trip of the Wabash Cannonball. One photographer chooses to use a 35mm still camera. The other will use a movie camera.

The Wabash Cannonball heads through the countryside and the still photographer waits at the Copper Canyon Bridge. When the Wabash arrives at the bridge, the still-photographer takes a snapshot of the train. This is a picture of the Wabash Cannonball at one moment in time.

The movie photographer, on the other hand, travels alongside the train and films it from the time it leaves the station until it arrives at the Copper Canyon Bridge. This is a picture of the train over a period of time.

The still photograph that was taken at the bridge represents the balance sheet. It is a picture of the Wabash at one moment in time. The balance sheet is a picture of a business at one moment in time—at the end of a period. It shows how many assets the business has, how much it owes, and how much the owner(s) have put into the business at a certain date.

The movie of the Wabash Cannonball from the station to the Copper Canyon Bridge is like an income statement. An Income Statement measures costs and expenses against sales revenues over a period of time. It shows the operation of the business and the profit over an *entire period.*

Since the balance sheet is a statement of one momen in time, it is headed with the date. For example:

W.T. Technologies
Statement of Financial Condition
January 31, 1980

The income statement, on the other hand, is for a continuous period ending on the date of the financial statement. Therefore, the income statement date is prefaced with the words "for the period ending . . ." For example:

W.T. Technologies
Income Statement
For the Six Month Period Ending January 31, 1980

The statement of retained earnings and the funds flow statement are not used as much as the balance sheet and income statement and most small businesspeople know very little about them. The IRS does *not* require the statement of retained earnings or funds flow statement to be included in any business's income tax, but if your company has a CPA who is doing an audited statement (or sometimes even an unaudited statement), generally accepted accounting principles require him or her to include these financial statements.

Retained earnings is the amount of money that is *retained* from net profit to be put back into the business. Retained earnings is what's left over from net profit after tax, dividends, owner's draw, principal loan repayment, and other items are taken out. Funds are defined as either the amount of working capital (current assets minus current liabilities) or cash.

By stretching the Wabash Cannonball example you can get an idea of what the statement of retained earnings and the funds flow statement measures in a business. Assume that the train has a certain amount of coal to stoke the engine when it starts out. Every so often along the track it stops to pick up more coal as the supply gets low. The coal is constantly burned up and has to be replaced. Besides using the coal for running the engine, the engineer may use the coal to heat the train or he may carve statues out of the coal for the tourist trade.

At the beginning of the train trip, the Wabash has a certain amount of coal and along the route it picked up some more. During the trip it used coal and at the end of the trip it will have a certain amount of coal left over. The engineer keeps an account book summarizing all the sources and uses of coal.

The statement of retained earnings and the funds flow statement are like the engineer's account book. Instead of coal, a business uses cash, working capital, and long-term capital. The statements are a summary of the sources and uses of cash, working capital, and long-term capital.

Throughout this book the six groups of accounts—assets, liabilities, equity, revenue (income), expenses, and cost of sales—have been discussed. Naturally these account groups are used in the financial statements. Assets, liabilities, and equity are the three basic account groups in the *balance sheet*. Income, expense, and cost of sales are the basic account groups in the *income statement*.

The statement of retained earnings or the funds flow statement is the measurement of the sources of business funds and the uses of those funds. It uses both the balance sheet and the income statement accounts.

The Income Statement

An income statement, commonly called a "profit and loss statement," consists of income, cost of sales, and expense accounts. *Gross margin*, or *gross profit* (the difference between income and cost of sales), and *net profit* (the difference between gross profit and operating expenses) are income statement amounts that are calculated.

A graphic presentation of an income statement can be seen in Figure 9.1. The accounts used—income, cost of sales, and operating expense—have amounts that come directly from the company's books (see Figure 9.2). By subtracting cost of sales from income, the result is the gross margin. If you subtract the operating expense from the gross margin the result is net profit. An income statement is usually presented in the following format.

Income	
Less:	Cost of sales
Equals:	Gross margin
Less:	Operating expense
Equals:	Net profit

Example. W.T. Technologies has $100,000 in sales for the year. They have $60,000 in costs of sales and $30,000 in operating expense. Their income statement would be calculated as follows:

Sales	$100,000
Less: Cost of sales	60,000
Equals: Gross margin	40,000
Less: Operating expense	30,000
Equals: Net profit	$ 10,000

You can also see from Figure 9.1 that some costs, such as taxes, principal loan repayment, and owner's salary or dividends, come out of net profit. Whatever is left after these costs are deducted from net profit becomes *retained earnings* which is part of the owner's equity on the balance sheet.

Figures 9.3, 9.4, 9.5, and 9.6 show a cross section of income statements from various industries. Notice that for the Monar Company, the income statement (profit and loss statement) in Figure 9.3 shows a retail store which has only one figure for cost of sales. The Wald Wholesale Company—a wholesaler (see Figure 9.4)—has a more complex statement of cost of goods sold. They include beginning inventory, purchases, freight and ending inventory in their cost of sales. The Hayes Manufacturing Company (Figure 9.5) has a cost of sales that is even more complex. For this reason, they included a separate cost of goods schedule (Figure 9.6).

Income statements of various industries differ primarily in their reporting of cost of sales. Service industries generally have *no* cost of sales whereas retail, wholesale, and manufacturing firms have cost of sales.

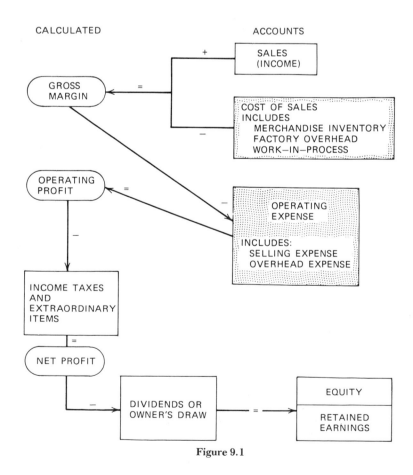

Figure 9.1

THE ACCOUNTS CIRCLE

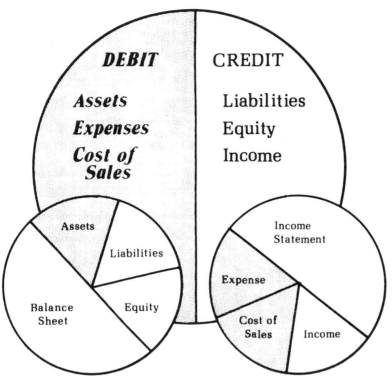

Figure 9.2

The MONAR Company
Profit and Loss Statement
For the Year Ended December 31, 19——

Sales		$120,000
Cost of goods sold		70,000
Gross margin		$50,000
Selling expenses		
Salaries	$15,000	
Commission	5,000	
Advertising	5,000	
Total selling expenses		25,000
Selling margin		$25,000
Administrative expenses		10,000
Net profit		$15,000

Figure 9.3

Wald Wholesale Company
Profit and Loss Statement
For the Year Ended December 31, 19——

Net sales			$666,720
Cost of goods sold			
Beginning inventory, January 1, 19——		$184,350	
Merchandise purchases	$454,920		
Freight and drayage	30,210	485,130	
Cost of goods available for sale		$669,480	
Less ending inventory December 31, 19——		193,710	
Cost of goods sold			475,770
Gross margin			$190,950
Selling, administrative, and general expenses			
Salaries and wages		$88,170	
Rent		24,390	
Light, heat, and power		8,840	
Other expenses		21,300	
State and local taxes and licenses		5,130	
Depreciation and amortization on leasehold improvements		4,140	
Repairs		2,110	
Total selling, administrative, and general expenses			154,080
Profit from operations			$36,870
Other income		$7,550	
Other expense		1,740	5,810
Net profit before taxes			$42,680
Provision for income tax			15,120
Net profit after income tax			$27,560

Figure 9.4

Income Statement Accounts. The income statement is made up of three groups of accounts: income, cost of sales, and expenses.

Income includes:

Income from the sales of merchandise
Rental income
Interest income
Investment income (dividends, etc.)
Income from sales of services

Cost of sales (cost of goods sold) is the total price paid for the products during the accounting period. Most retail and wholesale businesses compute cost of goods sold by adding the value of the goods purchased during the period to the beginning inventory, and then subtracting the ending inventory. Manufacturing firms include such items as factory overhead, direct labor, and the like, in their cost of sales (see Chapter 8). Cost of sales includes:

Merchandise inventory—finished and work-in-process
Raw materials
Factory overhead

Hayes Manufacturing Company
Profit and Loss Statement
For the Year Ended December 31, 19——

Net sales			$669,100
Cost of goods sold			
Finished goods inventory, January 1, 19——		$69,200	
Cost of goods manufactured (exhibit 6)		569,700	
Total cost of goods available for sale		$638,900	
Less finished goods inventory, Dec. 31, 19——		66,400	
Cost of goods sold			572,500
Gross margin			$96,600
Selling and administrative expenses			
Selling expenses			
Sales, salaries and commissions	$26,700		
Advertising expense	12,900		
Miscellaneous selling expense	2,100		
Total selling expenses		$41,700	
Administrative expenses			
Salaries	$27,400		
Miscellaneous administrative expense	4,800		
Total administrative expenses		32,200	
Total selling and administrative expenses			73,900
Net operating profit			$22,700
Other revenue			15,300
Net profit before taxes			$38,000
Estimated income tax			12,640
Net profit after income tax			$25,360

Figure 9.5

Hayes Manufacturing Company
Statement of Cost of Goods Manufactured
For the VEAR Ended December 31, 19——

Work-in-process inventory, January 1, 19——			$18,800
Raw materials			
Inventory, January 1, 19——		$154,300	
Purchases		263,520	
Freight In		9,400	
Cost of materials available for use		$427,220	
Less inventory, December 31, 19——		163,120	
Cost of materials used		$264,100	
Direct labor		150,650	
Manufacturing overhead			
Indirect labor	$23,750		
Factory heat, light, and power	89,500		
Factory supplies used	22,100		
Insurance and taxes	8,100		
Depreciation of plant and equipment	35,300		
Total manufacturing overhead		178,750	
Total manufacturing costs			593,500
Total work in process during period			$612,300
Less work-in-process inventory, December 31, 19——			42,600
Cost of goods manufactured			$569,700

Figure 9.6

Freight in
Other material purchases
Subcontract work
Factory salaries and labor

Operating expense includes general and administrative, selling, and shipping expenses, although sometimes businesses list these groups of expenses separately. General and administrative expense (sometimes simply called G&A) includes utilities, salaries, supplies, rents, and other operating costs necessary to the overall administration of the business. Selling expense includes salaries of the sales force, commissions, advertising expense, and so on. Other activities which contribute to the company sales activities can be shares of rent, heat, light, power, supplies, and other items. Operating expense includes:

Wages and salaries
Rental expense
Repairs and maintenance
Depreciation
Bad debt
Travel and transportation
Business entertainment
Interest
Insurance
Taxes
Licenses
Utilities
Supplies
Advertising
Charitable contributions
Accounting, legal, and consulting

Educational expenses for employees of the company
Some businesses receive additional income from interests, dividends, miscellaneous sales, rents, royalties, gains on sales of assets, and so on. In these cases, the net profit shown is really net operating profit and is referred to as such. The "other income" will be added to the net operating profit and any "extraordinary costs," such as loss on sales of assets, will be subtracted from it.

Statement of Financial Condition

A statement of financial condition (balance sheet) is a summary of what a business owns (assets) and what claims there are against those assets (liabilities, or creditors' claim, and equity, the owner's claim).

The balance sheet is the financial summary in the form of the basic accounting equation

$$assets = liabilities + equity$$

The balance sheet is based on historical costs. Assets are stated on the balance sheet at their original cost less any depreciation. Common and preferred stock is recorded at the original amount received for the stock. Liabilities are recorded at the amount presently (at the end of that accounting period) owed.

The reason for using historical cost is that it reduces to a minimum the extent to which the accounts are affected by the personal opinions of the owners. For example, if the value of assets was set at the present market value, the people responsible for the accounts would have to appraise the current market value. Of course, different people have entirely different ideas about what market value is. Therefore, if market value was used, two companies with identical forklifts might carry that asset at $1000 in one case and $10,000 in another.

Balance Sheet Examples.   Figure 9.7 shows the three account groups that make up the balance sheet: assets, liabilities, and equity. Notice that there is no computation required in a balance sheet as there is in an income statement. The statement is fully represented by the accounts on the books. Notice from the illustration that "retained earnings" from the income statement is incorporated into the equity position.

Figure 9.8 is a sample balance sheet of Fatcat, Inc. This illustration shows the typical categories and items of a balance sheet. Assets are on the left (or presented first) and Liabilities and Equity are on the right (or presented last). The first items of assets are the current assets. The first items presented in liabilities are the current liabilities. Current assets are assets that can be converted to cash within one year. Current liabilities also reflect a one year period, but they are debts which must be repaid within the next year.

Current assets are followed by a group of assets called "fixed assets" and by another group called "other assets." Fixed assets are assets which will remain for more than one year and generally (with the exception of land) are depreciable or amortizable assets. Other assets are not owned by every company. They are assets that cannot be converted to cash within one year and are generally not depreciable or amortizable. Some other assets, such as patents and intangibles, are amortized.

Following current liabilities are "long-term liabilities." Long-term liabilities are debts that will take more than one year to pay off. In accounting, more than one year is considered "long-term."

The equity (or capital) portion of the balance sheet shows the basic components of the owners' investment and retention of capital in the business: stock, paid-in surplus, and retained earnings. In proprietorships and partnerships, this section may just contain the owners' cumulative equity in the business (owners' equity) and the retained earnings for that period (sometimes just stated as "net profit").

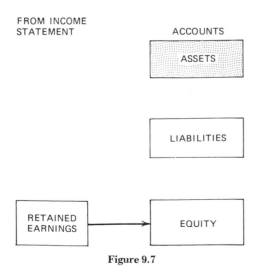

FROM INCOME
STATEMENT

ACCOUNTS

ASSETS

LIABILITIES

RETAINED
EARNINGS

EQUITY

Figure 9.7

Fatcat, Inc.
Balance Sheet
December 31, 198X

Assets

Current assets

Cash	$ 12,000	
Accounts receivable	119,000	
Notes receivable	7,800	
Inventories at cost (LIFO)	235,200	
Prepaid assets	26,000	
Total current assets		$ 400,000

Fixed assets

Land	45,000	
Buildings and improvements	230,000	
Equipment and vehicles	497,000	
Furniture and fixtures	31,456	
Less: Accumulated depreciation	(212,456)	
Total fixed assets		$ 591,000

Other assets

Investment in subsidiaries	49,000	
Goodwill	76,000	
Research and development	82,000	
Less: R&D amortization	(51,000)	
Total other assets		$ 156,000
Total assets		$1,147,000

Liabilities

Current liabilities

Accounts payable	$ 98,500	
Notes payable	7,340	
Accrued taxes	103,182	
Accrued salaries	10,340	
Provision for pensions	56,300	
Total current liabilities		$ 275,662

Long-term liabilities:

Notes payable	28,503	
Bonds (8½% due 1985)	310,635	
Total long-term liabilities		$ 339,138
Total liabilities		$ 611,800

Equity

Capital stock	100,000	
Paid-in surplus	120,000	
Retained earnings	315,200	
Total equity		$ 535,200
Total liabilities and equity		$1,147,000

Figure 9.8

Balance Sheet Accounts. An *asset* is property that is used in the trade of business. This property contributes toward earning the income of the business, either directly or indirectly. Assets are productive items which contribute to income and are generally tangible property or promises of future receipt of cash (accounts receivable, investments, etc). For a fuller discussion of assets, see Chapter 5.

Liabilities include all debt of the company, amounts of money owed but not yet paid. See Chapter 6 for a detailed discussion.

Equity (capital) is the amount of money that the owners have invested in the company. This includes the amount they started the company with (initial capital) plus all money that has accumulated in the company since its inception. See Chapter 7 for a detailed discussion.

Statement of Retained Earnings and Funds Flow statement

The statement of retained earnings is concerned with determining retained earnings at the end of a period. The funds flow statement includes the results of the statement of retained earnings, but it *also* goes further by tracking down every movement of cash during the period.

The statement of retained earnings shows the retained earnings at the beginning of a period, the adjustments to retained earnings during the period, and the retained earnings calculated for the end of the period.

The purpose of the funds flow statement is to trace the flow of working capital during the accounting period.

Neither statement is required for income tax purposes, but one or the other or both are required by "generally accepted accounting principles" set down by the American Institute of Certified Public Accountants (AICPA), the rule-making body of American CPAs. Politically held companies are generally required to have these statements as part of their financial reporting procedures.

Statement of Retained Earnings. Most corporations are required to show their retained earnings in a "statement of retained earnings." This financial statement shows the retained earnings at the beginning of the period (the end of the *last* period), adjustments made during the accounting period, and what the retained earnings are at the end of the present period.

Adjustments made during the period include:

1. Profit or loss from period after taxes.
2. Dividends or owner's draw.
3. Principal loan repayment.
4. Adjustments, charges, or credits resulting from transactions in the company's own capital stock (buying treasury stock or selling stock).
5. Transfers to and from accounts properly designated as appropriated retained earnings such as contingency reserves or provisions for replacement costs of fixed assets.
6. Adjustments made pursuant to a quasi-reorganization. See Figure 9.9 for an example and Figure 9.10 for a diagram.

	For the Years Ending	
	Dec. 31, 1979	Dec. 31, 1980
Retained earnings at beginning of the period	$100,320	$212,431
Net income for period	112,111	157,900
Common stock dividend—5% (4320 shares and $435 cash for partial shares)	-0-	$ 43,645
Retained earnings at end of period	$212,431	$326,696

Figure 9.9

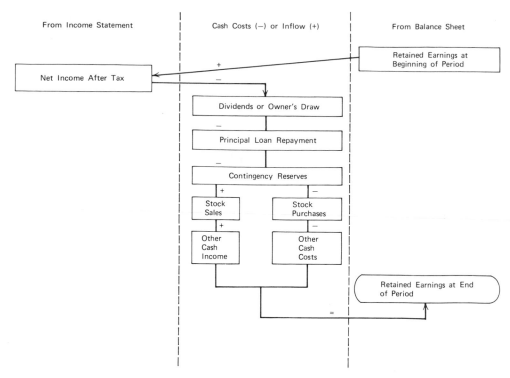

Figure 9.10

The Funds Flow Statement. Publically held companies are now required to have a funds flow statement along with their income statement and balance sheet. This statement traces the flow of working capital during the accounting period. Working capital is the excess of current assets over current liabilities.

The funds flow statement answers some of the following questions:

1. Where did profits go?
2. Why were dividends not larger in view of the profits made?
3. How was it possible to distribute dividends when the company had an net operating loss?
4. How was the expansion in plant and equipment financed?
5. What happened to the sale of additional stock and the proceeds from the sale of fixed assets?
6. How was the retirement of debt accomplished?
7. What brought about the increase or decrease in working capital?

Figure 9.11 shows how the funds flow statement can be divided into sources of funds (working capital) and application (uses) of funds. Notice that working capital is a *source* of funds when there is (1) an *increase* in liabilities or owner's equity or (2) a *decrease* in fixed assets. Funds are used *(applied)* when there is (1) a *decrease* in liabilities or owner's equity or (2) an *increase* in fixed assets.

Examples of sources of funds are loans and mortgages, injection of ownership cash into the business (stock or owner's injection), or increase in retained earnings from the previous year (from statement of retained earnings). Funds sources also include a decrease in fixed assets such as sales of equipment and other fixed assets and the ongoing depreciation expense.

Sources of Funds	Application of Funds

Increase in liabilities
  Loans
  Mortgages
	Decrease in liabilities
	  Pay-off loans
	  Pay-off mortgages

Increase in owner's equity:
  Owner cash injection
  Stock sales
  Increase in retained earnings
	Decrease in owner's equity
	  Withdrawals by owners
	  Decrease in retained earnings
	  Net loss

Decrease in fixed assets
  Sale of fixed assets
  Depreciation
	Increase in fixed assets
	  Purchase equipment, furniture
	    and fixtures, land and
	    building and leasehold
	    improvements

Figure 9.11. Funds flow statement.

Funds are used (applied) by paying off loans and mortgages (decreasing liabilities), withdrawals by owners through dividends or owner's draw, or by decreases in retained earnings resulting from net losses or large nonoperating cash expenditures. Funds are also used by increasing fixed assets such as purchase of equipment, buildings, and so on (see Figure 9.12).

Pete Popstein stopped. "That's about it. All that's left for me to do is to take your books to the office and complete your own statements. Are there any questions?"

Lazarus Time and Ignatz Whiz paused for a while and then shook their heads. Lazarus said "Let me try to repeat what you've said and see if I got it all right."

"Okay," Pete replied.

"A business has three accounting statements: the income statement, the balance sheet, and the statement of retained earnings.

"These financial statements are sort of like footprints of the business. From a dollar standpoint, they show where the business has been and where it is now.

"The income statement is the one that is required from all businesses by the IRS. It shows what the company's sales have been and what the expenses and net profit are.

Acme Mousetraps, Inc.
Funds Statement
For the Period Ending December 31, 197X

Source of funds		
Operations		
Net income	$25,316	
Add depreciation	5,720	$31,036
Sale of stock		10,000
Total sources		$41,036
Use of funds		
Purchase of fixed assets	$ 4,750	
Cash dividends paid	10,000	
Retirement of long-term debt	17,812	$32,562
Net increase in working capital		$ 8,474

Figure 9.12   Sample funds flow statement.

It is like a moving picture. It shows where the business has been from the beginning of the period to the end."

"Good," Pete commented.

"The balance sheet tells what a business owns and how much they owe against it. It also shows how much the owners have invested in the business. What you own is assets, what you owe is liabilities, and how much you have in it is equity. The balance sheet is like a still photograph; it tells what a business is like at one period in time.

"The statement of retained earnings shows the costs of a business that are cash cost, but not expenses—like owners' draw, dividends, principal loan repayment, and so on. It shows what happens to the net profit after tax."

"Good," Pete commented. "I think you understand. I'll see you in a few days." Pete looked at Laz and Ignatz, paused, and said goodbye.

Chapter Ten

From the Books
to the Financial Statements

The bottleneck at the Megatric holographic chip production plant was clearing up, Popstein was coming to W.T. Technologies with financial statements, and W.T. might soon have a loan. Things were looking up for Lazarus Time and Ignatz Culver Whiz.

Lazarus felt really good. He didn't even mind the exorbitant price that he knew Pete Popstein, the CPA, would charge them. It was worth it. And Lazarus started thinking that he was understanding accounting at last.

Ignatz and Laz were excited when Pete Popstein showed up for their meeting. "I've taken all your books and I've done a trial balance and prepared your financial statements. They look pretty good for the first six months.

"I'll start with the trial balance and tell you how the financial statements were put together." Pete leaned back as Laz and Ignatz looked at the documents lying in front of them. To make it easy, Pete had labeled each document.

THE TRIAL BALANCE AND THE ACCOUNTING WORKSHEET

Figure 10.1 shows the format of a trial balance sheet and company worksheet. Notice that there is a column for the account number (usually taken in numerical order) and one for the name of the account. The third and fourth columns are for recording the totals from each account in the general ledger.

The Trial Balance

The trial balance is made to test if the accounts properly balance. Total debits should equal total credits. Finding the equality of debits and credits is determined by finding the total balance in each account in the general ledger and by adding debit and credit balances separately to see if the totals are euqal.

The balance of an account is computed by (1) adding the figures on each side, then (2) subtracting the smaller total from the larger total to obtain the difference.

Using the cash account (account number 101) in Figure 10.2, first the debit side is added, and then the credit side. The total of each column is usually entered in pencil at the bottom of the column. These totals are called *footings*.

Adding up the debit column we see that the total cash taken in by the business adds up to $251,856. The total cash spent by the company in this period (cash credits)

YOUR COMPANY WORKSHEET

	ACCT. NO.	ACCOUNT NAME	TRIAL BALANCE 1 DEBIT	2 CREDIT
1				
2				
3				
4				
5				
6				
7				
8				
9				
10				
11				
12				
13				
14				
15				
16				
17				
18				
19				
20				
21				
22				
23				
24				
25				
26				
27				
28				
29				
30				

Figure 10.1

adds up to $248,300. Now, subtracting the smaller total (the credit balance of $248,300) from the larger total (the debit balance of $251,856) we get $3566. This number is the excess of the debit column over the credit column; therefore the account has a $3556 *debit* balance.

As you see in the example, this $3556 debit balance is written in pencil under the explanation column on the debit side.

No footings are required if the account only has one entry on one side or one entry on each side. The balance is simply written in the explanation space on the side (debit or credit) of the balance.

When the balances in each account are known, the accountant lists them in numerical order on the trial balance sheet. The totals from the accounts are placed in the proper column: debit balances are shown in the left column and credit balances are shown in the right column (see Figure 10.3).

CASH   # 101

DATE	ITEMS	Folio	√	DEBITS	DATE	ITEMS	Folio	√	CREDITS
1981					1981				
6/1	GJ 6-1			20000	6/6	GJ 6-4			3650
6/4	GJ 6-2			15000	6/10	GJ 6-5			3651
8/7	CRJ -1			124250	6/7	CDJ -1			6820
12/31	CRJ -2			92606	12/31	CDJ -2			234179
				251856					248300
	BALANCE			3556					

Figure 10.2

Note that the 100, 500, and 600 accounts (assets, expenses, and cost of sales) are all entered in the debit column because they all have debit balances. The 200, 300, and 400 accounts (liabilities, capital, and sales) are all entered in the credit column because they have credit balances.

After we have posted the trial balance and checked it for accuracy we can change the trial balance summary into the more usable form of an income statement and a balance sheet.

The Income Statement and Balance Sheet Workpaper Format

The trial balance extended for four more columns becomes the total workpaper. Notice in Figure 10.4 that debit and credit columns are added for both the income statement and the balance sheet. The columns marked "income statement" and "balance sheet" are used to organize the figures needed for these financial reports.

Accounts 100, 200, and 300 (the asset, liability, and equity accounts) are carried over to the balance sheet columns. Accounts 400, 500, and 600 (the income, expense, and cost of sales accounts) are carried over to the income statement columns. Accounts that had *debit* amounts in the trial balance will continue to be recorded as debits when transferred to the income statement or balance sheet columns. Accounts that are listed as *credits* in the trial balance will continue to be listed as credits in either the balance sheet or the income statement columns.

ACCT.	COMMENT	DEBIT	CREDIT
101	CASH	3556	
111	ACCOUNTS RECEIVABLE	119750	
111B	RESERVE FOR BAD DEBT		
115	INVENTORY		
120	PREPAID RENT	500	
122	TELEPHONE DEPOSIT	130	
125	RENTAL DEPOSIT	1400	
130	PROTOTYPE DEVELOPMENT	6388	
130A	AMORTIZATION OF PROTOTYPE		
140	LEASEHOLD IMPROVEMENTS	3651	
140D	DEPRECIATION OF LEASEHOLD IMP.		
201	ACCOUNTS PAYABLE		96500
210	NOTES PAYABLE - WHIZ		15000
301	EQUITY - LAZARUS TIME		13194
302	EQUITY - IGNATZ WHIZ		13194
410	HOLOGRAPHIC MEMORY SALES		327500
430	SUPPLY SALES		4200
440	REPAIR SERVICES		3600
508	RENTAL EXPENSE	3000	
509	RENTAL COMMISSION	1250	
510	TELEPHONE	1656	
511	SALES EXPENSE	3400	
515	OUTSIDE SERVICES	5200	
520	UTILITIES	685	
530	AUTO & DELIVERY	1710	
540	INSURANCE	1468	
550	ADVERTISING & PROMOTION	750	
560	OFFICE SUPPLIES	900	
570	ENTERTAINMENT	1970	
591	BUSINESS LICENSE	40	
595	OFFICERS SALARY AND TAXES	10000	
601	INVENTORY PURCHASES	75071	
610	SUB-CONTRACT	207213	
620	ENGINEERING	23500	
	TOTAL	473188	473188

Figure 10.3

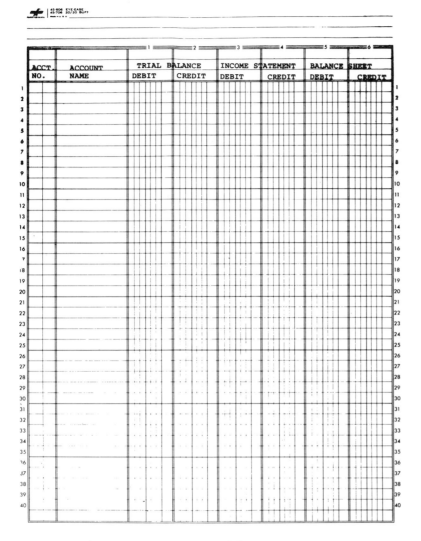

Figure 10.4

The total of the debit column is $473,188. The total of the credit column is also $473,188; thus both columsn balance (see Figure 10.3). This provides evidence that the original journal entries were made correctly.

If the debit and credit columns do not equal each other an error has been made. The following are some common errors:

1. Errors in addition
2. Recording only half an entry (the credit without the debit, or vice-versa)
3. Recording both halves of the entry on the same side (two debit or two credit entries rather than one debit and one credit)
4. Recording one or more accounts incorrectly.
5. Arithmetic errors in the journal entry.
6. Arithmetic errors in balancing the accounts.
7. Errors made by putting an entry in the wrong account.

One technique used by long-time bookkeepers to find out where the errors have occurred is to divide the difference between the debit side and the credit side by nine (9). If the amount of the difference is evenly divisible by 9, the discrepancy may either be a transposition ($432 for $423) or a slide ($423 for $42.30). Dividing the difference by two (2) may suggest the amount of a credit posted as a debit or vice versa.

"These are the completed workpapers for W.T. Technologies," Pete Popstein told Laz and Ignatz (see Figure 10.5). "Look at this carefully. You see that it has columns not only from the trial balance, but also for: (1) adjustments required to make the trial balance accurate; (2) an adjusted trial balance column, which is the total of the trial balance column and the adjustments column; (3) an income statement column, which is the one from which W.T.'s income statement comes; and (4) a balance sheet column, which represents the business's actual balance sheet from that period."

Pete Popstein paused as Lazarus Time and Ignatz Whiz looked at the completed worksheet.

Lazarus had a question: "Why all of these columns?"

"The first trial balance that you take is accurate as far as debits and credits go, but it ignores some expenses that are only calculated at the end of the period, such as depreciation, amortization, and bad debt. The trial balance also does not include the real cost of goods sold.

"In a business like consulting, you don't have any cost of goods sold, but in W.T. Technologies and all nonservice industries you will have cost of sales. This has to be determined at the end of the period by taking a physical inventory to see what is actually left. Some of the larger companies have a "perpetual" inventory system that keeps track of inventory on a constant basis. Since W.T. Technologies had only two machines—one complete and one partially complete—and some supplies, taking the inventory here was easy."

"At any rate," Pete Popstein continued, "you can see how the first trial balance isn't accurate. The first trial balance has to be adjusted. You can see that I put in adjustments for bad debt, amortization, depreciation, and inventory on the complete workpapers." (See Figure 10.5.)

Pete asked Laz, "Do you understand?"

"Yeah, I understand *what* you did but not *why*," Lazarus answered.

"Okay," the CPA answered, "I'll show you step by step what I did . . ."

COMPANY FINANCIAL STATEMENTS AND CLOSING ENTRIES

Income Statements and Balance Sheet

From the worksheet, the income statement and balance sheet columns can be put into a finalized format.

To create the *income statement* (see Figure 10.6) the income accounts, cost of sales accounts, expense accounts, and inventory adjustments are transferred from the worksheet.

To create the *balance sheet* (see Figure 10.7) the asset, liability, and equity accounts from the worksheet are used. The assets are on one side of the sheet of the paper and the liabilities and owner's equity are on the other side. The equation is represented as such

$$assets = liabilities + equity$$

W.T. Technologies – Worksheet
12/31/81

ACCT NO.	ACCOUNT NAME	TRIAL BALANCE Debit	TRIAL BALANCE Credit	ADJUSTMENTS Debit	ADJUSTMENTS Credit	ADJUSTED TRIAL BALANCE Debit	ADJUSTED TRIAL BALANCE Credit	INCOME STATEMENT Debit	INCOME STATEMENT Credit	BALANCE SHEET Debit	BALANCE SHEET Credit
101	Cash	3556				3556				3556	
111	Accounts Receivable	119750				119750				119750	
111B	Reserve for Bad Debt				(B)10059		10059				10059
115	Inventory								(C)126000	(C)126000	
140	Pre-paid rent	500				500				500	
142	Telephone Deposit	130				130				130	
125	Rental Deposits	1900				1900				1900	
130	Prototype Development	6388				6388				6388	
130A	Amortization				(A)300		300				300
140	Leasehold Improvements	3651				3651				3651	
140D	Depreciation				(A)121		121				121
201	Accounts Payable		96500				96500				96500
210	Notes Payable – Whiz		15000				15000				15000
301	Equity – Lazarus Tint		13194				13194				13194
302	Equity – Ignatz Whiz		13194				13194				13194
410	Holographic Memory Sales		329500				329500		329500		
430	Supply Income		4200				4200		4200		
440	Repair Services		3600				3600		3600		
508	Rental Expense	3000				3000		3000			
509	Rental Commission	1250				1250		1250			
510	Telephone	1656				1656		1656			
511	Sales Expense	3460				3460		3460			
515	Outside Services	5200				5200		5200			
520	Utilities	685				685		685			
530	Auto & Delivery	1710				1710		1710			
510	Insurance	1468				1468		1468			
550	Advertising & Promotion	250				250		250			
560	Office Supplies	900				900		900			
590	Entertainment	1990				1990		1990			
591	Business License	40				40		40			
595	Licensing Fees & Taxes	10000				10000		10000			
596	Bad Debt			(B)10059		10059		10059			
598	Depreciation and Amortization			(A)421		421		421			
601	Inventory Purchases	250071				250071		250071			
610	Sub-Contract	207213				207213		207213			
620	Engineering	23500				23500		23500			
	Total	4731588	4731588	10480	10480	4853668	4853668	345293	361300	161575	148368
	Net Profit							13007			13007
								361300	361300	161375	161375

Figure 10.5

W.T. Technologies
Income Statement
For the Period Ending December 31, 1981

Income		
Holographic memory machines	$375,500	
Supplies	4,200	
Repair	3,600	
Gross income		$383,300
Inventory purchases	75,071	
Subcontract	207,213	
Engineering	23,500	
Less: Ending inventory	(26,000)	
Less: Cost of goods sold		$279,784
Gross income		103,516
Operating expense		
Rental expense and commission	4,250	
Telephone and utilities	2,341	
Sales expense	3,400	
Outside services	5,200	
Auto and delivery	1,710	
Insurance	1,468	
Advertising and promotion	750	
Officer supplies	900	
Entertainment	1,970	
Business license	40	
Officers salary and taxes	10,000	
Bad debt	10,059	
Depreciation and amortization	421	
Total operating expense		$ 42,509
Net profit		$ 61,007

Figure 10.6

Note that in the equity section of the balance sheet the net profit is added to the owner's original equity which equals the new owner's equity. Also note that the allowance for bad debt is used to reduce the accounts receivable, and the allowance for amortization and allowance for depreciation are used to reduce the value of the prototype development and leasehold improvements.

Adjustments to Accounts

Before you add up the accounts and summarize them, there are some expenses that have to be calculated that only occur at the end of an accounting period. Depreciation, amoritzation, and bad debt expense must be calculated. All businesses that do not have a "perpetual" inventory system must make a physical count of inventory.

At the end of the period, the following is usually true:

1. Equipment, land, fixtures, and other assets such as prototype development are carried in their accounts at their original cost without regard for the usual wear and tear during the period or their salvage value.
2. The amount in the accounts receivable account might include some money that will not be collected in the future.
3. If you own a business that is other than service oriented, there is no recognition of merchandise you have in inventory that has not been sold by the end of the period.

W.T. Technologies
Statement of Financial Conditions
December 31, 1981

Assets

Current assets:

Cash		$ 3,556	
Accounts receivable	$119,750		
Less allowance for bad debt	10,050	109,691	
Inventory		26,000	
Prepaids and deposits		2,030	
Total current assets			$141,277

Fixed and other assets

Leasehold improvements	3,651		
Less depreciation	121	3,530	
Prototype development	6,388		
Less amortization	300	6,088	
Total fixed and other assets			9,618
Total assets			$150,895

Liabilities and Equity

Liabilities

Accounts payable		96,500	
Note payable—Whiz 10%		879	
Total current liabilities			97,379
Note payable—Whiz long-term		14,121	
Total long-term Liabilities			14,121
Total liabilities			$111,500

Owners Equity

Time equity	13,194		
Whiz equity	13,194	26,388	
Net profit 12/31/81		13,007	
Total owners equity			39,395
Total liabilities and equity			$150,895

Figure 10.7

DEPRECIATION

In reality, W.T.'s prototype development and leasehold improvements experience wear and tear. Accounting logic and the tax authorities allow this wear and tear to be taken into consideration and listed as an expense. This expense is called "depreciation." Depreciation is unusual in that it is not a cash expense. It is an allowance for the decline in value of the equipment.

Because leasehold improvements do not lose all their value in one period, the loss in value is apportioned over a longer period—the useful life of the asset. The useful life of an asset is a period of years after which the asset will be useless to the company, and therefore, sold. The IRS has certain guidelines for different types of equipment and other assets in its *Publication 534*. Generally, auto equipment is depreciated between three and five years, other types of equipment averages about five to seven years useful life, and buildings and improvements have a useful life of between 15 and 20 years.

W.T. Technologies has two assets that can be depreciated or amortized. The difference between amortization and depreciation is one of name only. Depreciation is for equipment and other fixed assets. Amortization is for "other assets" such as organizational expense, prototypes, and the like. Amortization and depreciation are calculated in the same manner. They only differ in the *type* of assets for which they show wear and tear.

Let's take W.T.'s prototype development cost that is capitalized as an asset. It is an asset worth $6388. Let's assume that we can amortize it over a period of 10 years, and at the end of that time it will be worth $388 in junk parts value. In other words, it cost $6,388, will have a useful life of 10 years, and at the end of that ten years, it will have a "salvage value" of $388.

Amortization for prototype development is calculated as follows:

cost	minus	salvage value	equals	amortizable value
$6388	−	$388	=	$6000

amortizable value	divided by	useful life	equals	annual amortization
$6000	÷	10	=	$600

The leasehold improvements that you recorded may have depreciation calculated on them in a similar manner. W.T. Technologies' leasehold improvements belongs to the landlord when the lease expires in 15 years.

Depreciation for leasehold improvements is calculated as follows:

$$\$3651 - \$0 = \$3651 \text{ depreciable value}$$

$$\$3651 \div 15 \text{ years} = \$243.40, \text{ or } \$243 \text{ rounded annual depreciation}$$

When the period for which the books are being closed is *less than* one year, the depreciation expense must be adjusted to reflect depreciation for a period less than a year. In the W.T. example, the books are being closed for a six *months* period, therefore the amount of depreciation for the year must be divided by two because the depreciation is for only six months. The general formula would be as follows:

$$\frac{\text{total depreciation for year}}{\text{number of periods in the year}} = \text{depreciation for that period}$$

Annual depreciation and amortization	Divided by	Number of periods in year	=	Depreciation for period
Prototype	$600	÷	2	$300
Leasehold improvements	243	÷	2	121
Total	$843			$421

The depreciation for the period for W.T. Technologies is $421.

If the period were three months (one quarter) the total depreciation would be divided by four.

When depreciation and amortization are calculated, they are put in an adjustments column that is alongside the trial balance columns. Depreciation is entered in the adjustments column (see Figure 10.5) as a debit to depreciation and amortization expense (597) and a credit to allowance for depreciation (140 D) and allowance for amortization (130 A).

Note that in the example all three entries are labeled "(A)" so that they can be easily identified for future reference.

BAD DEBT EXPENSE

In business there is always the probability that some accounts receivables will *not* be collected.

There are two methods for determining bad debt loss. One method is to wait until the company is sure that the account of a specific customer is uncollectable, and then record the expense. An entry is made debiting a bad debt expense account and crediting the asset account, accounts receivable.

Another way to allow for this bad debt expense is to *anticipate* bad debt losses and provide for them ahead of time. This is called setting up an allowance for bad debt.

Bad debt losses are estimated as a percentage of total credit sales. In some industries bad debt loss might be 10% and in others it might run 1% of credit sales.

Using the industry experience if you are a new business, or past experience if you have been in business for some time, you can set up a bad debt account.

We can calculate what the bad debt allowance should be for W.T. Technologies. The industry generally experiences 3% loss on credit sales so we'll use that figure:

Credit sales for the six months	$335,300
Times estimated percentage bad debt loss	×.03
Estimated bad debts on January sales	$ 10,059

W.T.'s expected bad debt loss for June through December sales is $10,059 (3% of total credit sales of $335,300).

In Figure 10.5 bad debt allowance and expense is added to the adjustments column. The amount of bad debt for that month is debited to bad debt expense (596) and credited to allowance for bad debts (111B). The allowance for bad debt (111B) is a reduction in accounts receivable expected.

Note that the two entries are marked "(B)" for later identification.

At this point, all the adjustments for the adjustments column next to the trial balance columns have been made. We can now total the columns. Next we add three more sets of columns: the adjusted trial balance, income statement, and balance sheet (see Figure 10.5). The adjusted trial balance columns can now be filled out by adding the debit and credit columns of the trial balance with the adjustments. All the entries of the trial balance are now combined with the entries from adjustments.

INVENTORY AND COST OF SALES ADJUSTMENTS

From the time W.T. Technologies started six months ago, it has been purchasing materials and paying for engineering and subcontract work. The money that was spent represents not only the costs of producing the holographic memory machines, but also includes the cost of materials and machines that have not been sold yet.

In order to get a true picture of cost of sales, we must determine the value of the inventory left over at the end of the period. To do this a physical inventory must be taken. W.T. had this done last December, the end of the period.

Here are the steps to be taken:

1. The value of the merchandise that is unsold at the end of the period must be recorded as an addition to inventory (the asset).
2. The cost of the merchandise sold should be recorded as part of the cost of sales.

The physical inventory that W.T. took at the end of the period shows $26,000 in supplies and machines in inventory at the end of the period. W.T. also had inventory purchases of $75,071, subcontract payments of $207,213, and engineering costs of $23,500.

The adjustments to inventory are recorded directly on the income statement and balance sheet columns of the complete workpapers (Figure 10.5).

First, the value of the ending inventory of W.T. Technologies ($26,000) is recorded as a debit to the balance sheet column (the entry is marked "C" for later identification).

Secondly, a credit entry ($26,000) is made to the income statement column on the inventory line (this is also marked "C").

Entering the amount of the ending inventory as a credit entry to the income statement column has the effect of reducing the cost of sales by the amount of inventory that was not sold (ending inventory).

The entry of the ending inventory ($26,000) has the same effect as this cost of sales calculation:

Beginning inventory		$ -0-
Plus:	Inventory purchases	75,071
	Subcontract	207,213
	Engineering	23,500
Less:	Ending inventory	26,000
Cost of goods sold		$279,784

Completing the Worksheet

The following steps are now taken to complete the worksheet (see Figure 10.5).

First, carry over the balances from assets, liabilities, and equity (100, 200, and 300 accounts) to the balance sheet.

Next, carry over the balances from income, expenses, and cost of sales (accounts 400, 500, and 600) to the income statement.

Then add up all the columns. The income statement and the balance sheet will have different amounts in the debit and in the credit column. This difference represents W.T.'s net profit. On the income statement the debit column (expenses and cost of sales) adds up to $348,293 and the credit column (income) adds up to $361,300. The differences between the two Figures is $13,007. This amount represents the net profit and is added to the debit side to bring the columns in balance. Similarly, the balance sheet debit and credit columns do not balance when they are first added up, but if the $13,007 net profit from the income statement is carried over and entered in the credit column, the totals will both add up to $161,375. This is because net profit is actually an addition to owner's equity.

Especially notice that in the liability section of the statement of financial condition (balance sheet) (Figure 10.7) the note that is owed to I.C. Whiz of $15,000 is divided into a current portion (the amount of principal due within one year) and a long-term portion (the amount of money due *after* one year).

We assumed that Whiz loaned money to the partnership at 10% which is the maximum personal rate in this state and that the note would be paid back in 10 years. The note to Whiz will be paid off at $2379 per year interest and principal. The principal portion of that debt is $879. Therefore, the current portion of the long-term debt is $879. The long-term portion of the note is $14,121 ($15,000 loaned less $879 paid in the first year).

"Well, do you see how it all works? I've got something else for you," Pete Popstein said to Laz and Ignatz. "It is a chart that shows the form of the income statement and the balance sheet." (See Figure 10.8.)

	Income Statement	Balance Sheet
Heading	(Name of Company) Income statement For (#) month(s) Ending (date)	(Name of Company) Balance sheet (date)
Layout	One column lists sales, then cost of sales, gross profit, operating expenses, then net profit.	Two columns going down the page— assets listed on the right side and liabilities and equity listed on the left side. Liabilities are listed on the left side before equity.
Underlining	Single lines should be drawn *just above* the totals for income, cost of sales, gross profit, total operating expense, and net profit.	Single lines should be drawn *just above* the totals for current assets, fixed assets, and total assets; current liabilities, long-term liabilities, total liabilities, total equity, and total liabilities and equity. A *double* line should be drawn *under* total assets and total liabilities and assets.

Figure 10.8

"Well, is that all of what happens in accounting?" Ignatz asked Pete.

"The last thing is that you close your books for the period," Pete replied. "The whole end-of-period process requires several steps (shown in Figure 10.9). I'll explain it step by step."

"The first step is to determine the debit or credit balances in each of the ledger accounts. This is done by adding both columns in each account and finding the difference (subtracting one from the other). The column which has the highest total will have this difference written in the explanation space." (See Figure 10.2.)

"Step two requires the balance in each account to be entered in either the debit or credit column of a trial balance worksheet, depending on whether it is a debit or credit balance in the ledger account." (See Figure 10.3.)

"Step three is to adjust for depreciation and bad debt in the adjusted trial balance columns in the worksheet.

"Step four is to extend the trial balance figures over to the adjusted trial balance.

"Step five extends all the totals from the adjusted trial balance to the income statement and balance sheet columns.

"Step six is to make all the closing entries in the general journal and the ledgers."

Pete looked around the room. "I'll go now. If there's anything else I can do for you let me know. I would like to be your permanent accountant."

Lazarus Time and Ignatz Whiz thanked Pete and sat down and split a bottle of champagne. Lazarus would make an appointment with the bank for a loan the next day.

STEP	ACTION
1	TOTAL DEBIT AND CREDIT BALANCES IN ALL ACCOUNTS
2	ENTER ACCOUNT BALANCES IN TRIAL BALANCES
3	ADJUST FOR DEPRECIATION AND BAD DEBT ON ADJUSTED TRIAL BALANCE
4	EXTEND TRIAL BALANCE FIGURES TO ADJUSTED TRIAL BALANCE
5	MAKE INVENTORY ADJUSTMENTS TO INCOME STATEMENT AND BALANCE SHEET COLUMNS OF WORKSHEET
6	EXTEND TOTALS FROM ADJUSTED TRIAL BALANCE COLUMNS TO INCOME STATEMENT AND BALANCE SHEET COLUMNS
7	MAKE ALL CLOSING ENTRIES IN GENERAL JOURNAL AND LEDGERS

Figure 10.9

Chapter Eleven
Business Finance and Ratios

Lazarus Time looked at the W.T. Technologies balance sheet and income statement. He hoped this would make the banker decide in his favor for a $50,000 loan.

W.T. needed about $40,000 in new equipment and about $10,000 in working capital and inventory. W.T. Technologies had made a profit even though they had only been in business for about eight months.

Lazarus Time met with Mr. Pumiceheart again. He gave the banker his financial statements and talked to the banker about his request for $50,000. Pumiceheart seemed to listen, but all the time he was running his eyes over the business's financial statements.

Pumicchcart took the financial statements and told Laz that he could consider the loan and let him know in the next two days. Laz got the impression that it wasn't going to go too well.

Three days later Laz and Ignatz received a letter declining the loan. When Laz called Pumiceheart to see what the problem was, Pumiceheart said, "The ratios are not acceptable for a loan under bank policy." Pumiceheart would not talk any more about it.

That night was the last accounting class at the university extension. Laz arrived at the class a little early so he could talk to the instructor. Laz told the instructor about the loan decline and asked him what he thought.

The instructor thoughtfully stroked the collar of his Hawaiian print shirt. "Banks have certain rules about what kind of businesses they can loan money to. The only way that banks make decisions logically about a loan is by using certain financial ratios.

"When the banker talked to you about ratios," the instructor continued, "he was talking about debt to worth ratios, current ratios and other 'tools' that banks use to decide if your business is strong enough to make the loan repayment. The bank itself has rules about what these ratios should look like. This is usually printed in what is called an 'operation manual'. In that manual it might say that a business in your industry that is as old as you are should have a debt-to-worth ratio of 1 to 3 after the loan. If your debt-to-worth ratio is now 3, for instance, and will be 5 after the loan, then the bank cannot loan to you.

"There is a lot more to it than this, of course," the instructor continued. "There may be certain collateral requirements, and so on. But one thing you can be sure of—if the bank officer decided to approve your loan, he or she would have to do all kinds of ratios and comparisons to justify it to the bank and the bank examiners."

The teacher looked up at the clock. "It's time to start the class now. I'm going to cover some of these ratios tonight. If you want some more explanation later, see me after the class."

The instructor looked at the class and began. . . .

Accounting information is the basic data of business. It shows how much you make, what you spent, what you own, what you owe, and how much the owners' have in the business. But by itself accounting information has no predictive or deductive qualities. It does not show you how to control operating expenses, to grant credit intelligently, to understand basic inventory relationships, and to manage cash flow. Finance is the art of gathering accounting information and making predictions and deductions from it as to how your business can improve and what the problem areas are. It takes the raw accounting data and makes judgements about how this compares to a typical situation and how this compares to the history of the business.

FINANCIAL STATEMENTS AND FINANCE

Of themselves, a balance sheet and income statement are a collection of inanimate figures. But when the assorted financial symbols are interpreted and evaluated, they begin to talk.

A single balance sheet is like the opening chapters of a book—it gives the initial setting. Thus, one balance sheet will show how the capital is distributed, how much is in the various accounts, and how much surplus of assets over liabilities exists. A lone income statement indicates the sales volume for a given period, the amount of costs incurred, and the amount earned after allowing for all costs.

When a series of balance sheets for regularly related intervals—such as fiscal or calendar year ends—is arranged in vertical columns so that related items may be compared, the changes in these items begin to disclose trends. The comparative balance sheets then no longer remain snapshots, but are converted into X-rays, penetrating outer tissue and outlining the skeletal structure of all basic management actions and decisions.

Comparative profit and loss statements reveal significant changes in what took place in the business. Were prices cut to meet competition? Then look for a lower gross profit—unless purchasing costs were reduced proportionately. Did sales go up? If so, what about expenses? Did they remain proportionate? Was more money spent on office help? Where did the money come from? How about fixed overhead? Was it controlled? It is only by comparing operating income and cost account items from one period to another that revealing answers can be found.

Uses of Finance

The areas where most businesspeople use finance are:

1. To control and predict collections of accounts receivable.
2. To control and predict inventory movement and depletion.
3. To control operations.
4. To manage finances including borrowing money and selling business ownership.

What type of financial ratios and other tools a businessperson uses depends on which of these four areas needs to be analyzed. For instance, if the business is having cash flow problems because they are *not* collecting on receivables, collection financial tools are the most important. A financial tool to help in collections is the *accounts receivable period ratio*. This ratio tells a business what its average collection is.

In order to make this chapter more practical for the average reader-businessperson, we will cover the ratios in general then cover the specially applicable ratios for each general use: collections, inventory, operations, and financial management.

BASIC INFORMATION ON RATIOS

All ratios are based on the balance sheet and income statement. Ratios are computed in one of the following ways:

1. Only balance sheet numbers are used to show relations between the various balance sheet items.
2. Only income statement numbers are used to show their relationships.
3. Both the balance sheet and the income statement are used to show the relationship between an item on the income statement and on the balance sheet.

When you calculate ratios all you need is 10 numbers: seven from the balance sheet, two from the income statement, and one that is calculated by subtracting two balance sheet figures from each other. The figures you need are:

From the Balance Sheet
Total current assets
Accounts receivable
Inventory
Total fixed assets
Total current liabilities
Total all liabilities
Net worth

From the Income Statement
Net sales
Net profit after taxes

Calculated from Two Balance Sheet Items
Working capital (current assets minus current liabilities)

A primary objective in this chapter is to narrow down the field of ratios to a working minimum for business use. Because of this, a certain selection and rejection of material has obviously been necessary. The following ratios, for instance, reflect chiefly balance sheet relationships. A few combine balance sheet and profit and loss items, while one—net profit on net sales—is based exclusively on data from the profit and loss statement. The procedures for preparing an all-balance-sheet study follow the same pattern as those outlined in connection with combined balance-sheet and income-statement analyses.

The following nine ratios, organized by their applicable area of management, are the most practical for business:

Collections
1. Average collection period of receivables

Operations

  2. Net fixed assets to tangible net worth
  3. Net profit on net sales

Financial Management

  4. Current assets to current liabilities
  5. Current liabilities to tangible net worth
  6. Net Sales to tangible net worth
  7. Net sales to net working capital
  8. Net profits to tangible net worth
  9. Total debt to tangible net worth

Industry Ratios

It is a good idea not only to compute your company's ratios, but also compare them to your industry. Several industry ratio studies are available to the public.

Ratio sources may be classified into two groups: those agencies which compile data for a number of individual industries, and those which confine their work to a particular industry or a group of related industries. The best known of the former are Dun and Bradstreet, Inc., Robert Morris Associates, and The Accounting Corporation of America. The latter group is composed of trade associations, publishers of trade magazines, specialized accounting firms, industrial companies (e.g. National Cash Register Co.), and colleges and universities. In addition to these groups, Federal Government agencies provide a wealth of data covering somewhat broader industry classifications (in most cases) than the private sources.

FINANCIAL RATIOS FOR COLLECTIONS, OPERATIONS, INVENTORY, AND FINANCIAL MANAGEMENT

Figure 11.1 and Figure 11.2 are the income statements and balance sheet for two hypothetical companies: Hero Manufacturing and Rotten Distribution. Hero Manufacturing Company is a well managed company and all of their ratios look good. Rotten Distribution, on the otherhand, is a mismanaged company, and the illustrations of their ratios reflect this.

Hero Manufacturing is an iron and steel foundry, so for comparison we will use the Dun and Bradstreet *Key Business Ratios* for this industry. The second item in Figure 11.3, the *Key Business Ratios*, is for iron and steel foundries.

Rotten Distribution is a scrap and waste materials wholesaler. Their ratios are compared with Figure 11.4, a copy of the Dun and Bradstreet *Key Business Ratios* for wholesaling.

Collection Ratios

Of all the ratios, the most important may be the one which indicates how long many businesses, especially small businesses, run into cash flow problems. In about 70% of the cases, this cash flow problem is caused by not collecting receivables in a timely manner. Since customers will very seldom pay their invoices until they are reminded, and some companies won't pay unless you "stand on them," an effective collection policy is of the utmost importance to a business.

The collection period ratio will tell you if your customers are generally paying in the time they are allocated. If they are not paying, corrective action must be taken.

Collection Period. As any top manager can tell you, a company's credit and collections program and terms exert a direct influence on sales attainment, profits, and the need for borrowing capital. This ratio helps analyze the collectability of receivables. The average collection period should not exceed the net maturity indicated by selling terms by more than 10 to 15 days. This ratio is especially important today when accounts receivable is an increasingly major asset.

The collection period in days is determined by a two-step formula. The first step is to divide the *annual* credit sales by 365 days to obtain the average *daily* credit sales. If all the company's sales are on credit, the credit sales equal the total net sales. But if the company does a large portion of its business on a cash basis, the cash sales must be subtracted from net sales to get credit sales. The second step in the formula is to divide accounts and notes receivable by the average daily credit sales (the result of the first step calculation) to get the average collection period in days.

Step 1.

$$\text{average daily credit sales} = \frac{\text{total annual credit sales}}{365 \text{ days}}$$

Step 2.

$$\text{collection period in days} = \frac{\text{notes and accounts receivable}}{\text{average daily credit sales}}$$

Example.

Hero Manufacturing   Rotten Distribution

Step 1. $\dfrac{\$5,620,000^*}{365 \text{ days}} = \$15,397$ $\dfrac{\$4,200,000^*}{365 \text{ days}} = \$11,507$

Step 2. $\dfrac{\$\ 580,000}{15,397} = 37 \text{ days}$ $\dfrac{\$690,000}{11,507} = 60 \text{ days}$

Hero Manufacturing collects its receivables faster than anyone in the industry (industry best: 40 days; average: 48 days). The faster a company collects its receivables, the less likely its need for additional working capital. Rotten Distribution collects their receivables slower than anyone in the industry (48 days) and much slower than the average (36 days). This means that Rotten is going to require more working capital than anyone else in the industry and, since they have very little working capital now, they will have to borrow or go slow on their trade obligations.

Note. If the figures you have from your business are not annual figures, but interim figures, you must divide credit sales by the number of days in the period (183 days for two quarters, 90 days for one quarter, etc.). Dividing by 365 days is done only if you are using annual figures.

Operations Ratios

Operating ratios help you determine how well the operation of your business is. One ratio tells you how profitable your company is, the other ratio helps you determine if you have enough (or too much) invested in fixed assets.

Net Profit on Net Sales. The net profit to sales ratio is important for measuring the profitability of your business. Its ratio represents the net profit margin as a percentage of sales. It explains what percentage of sales the actual net profit is after taxes. Too

*All of Hero Manufacturing's and Rotten Distribution's sales are on credit.

	Hero Manufacturing		Rotten Distribution	
	Present Year 12/30/19X2	Previous Year 12/30/19X1	Present Year 12/30/19X2	Previous Year 12/30/19X1
Sales and Revenue				
Net sales of product	5,620,000	4,323,000	4,200,000	4,620,000
Interest income	51,750	40,100	-0-	-0-
Total income	5,671,750	4,363,100	4,200,000	4,620,000
Less: Cost of sales				
Merchandise	1,067,800	767,333	2,940,000	3,194,083
Wages	2,135,600	1,534,665	185,000	201,062
Factory overhead	640,680	460,399	65,000	70,594
Selling costs	427,120	306,933	212,000	230,261
Total cost of sales	4,271,200	3,069,330	3,402,000	3,696,000
Gross profit	1,400,550	1,293,770	798,000	924,000
Operating expense				
Wages, general	400,000	380,000	400,000	420,000
Officers' Wages	80,000	70,000	N/A	N/A
Payroll tax	43,200	40,500	43,200	48,700
Insurance	90,000	82,000	45,300	47,000
Accounting and legal	42,000	36,000	25,000	27,000
Administrative costs	85,000	81,000	10,446	22,200
Supplies and postage	3,500	3,200	5,000	6,100
Rent for premises	65,000	55,000	26,000	26,000
Utilities and phone	7,200	6,900	12,010	11,600
Travel and entertainment	41,700	40,900	63,000	74,200
Leases	28,000	24,000	12,200	10,900
Tax and license	3,800	3,200	2,600	2,700
Dues and subscriptions	4,500	4,600	3,100	3,700
Depreciation and amortization	3,000	2,900	1,700	1,700
Interest	65,779	71,460	176,444	90,200
Commissions	39,140	30,110	-0-	-0-
Total operating expense	991,823	921,770	756,000	792,000
Net profit	408,727	372,000	42,000	132,000

Less reserve for taxes	183,927	167,400	12,600	52,800
Adjusted net profit	224,800	204,600	29,400	79,200

Cost of Sales Schedule

Merchandise

Furnished goods inventory—beginning	176,000	145,320	551,300	550,200
Work in process inventory—beginning	95,000	78,311	N/A	N/A
Raw material inventory—beginning	115,000	94,503	N/A	N/A
Material purchases	991,000	817,829	2,875,890	3,153,583
Freight in	21,100	17,300	32,100	41,600
Less:	90,300	115,000	N/A	N/A
Less: Finished goods ending	150,000	176,000	583,310	551,300
Less: Work-in-process	90,300	95,000	N/A	N/A
Total cost of materials	1,067,800	767,333	2,940,000	3,194,083

Direct Labor Costs

Factory salaries	1,312,260	939,216	107,000	119,000
Shipping salaries	498,000	356,042	55,000	59,000
Payroll tax and benefits	161,113	118,169	16,200	17,800
Bonus and vacation	164,227	121,238	6,800	5,262
Total direct labor costs	2,135,600	1,534,665	185,000	201,062

Factory overhead

Rent and equipment leases	320,000	280,000	25,800	25,800
Utilities	93,133	39,399	1,200	1,300
Supplies	60,000	56,000	4,000	6,000
Repairs and maintenance	57,000	43,000	5,000	11,494
Equipment depreciation	110,547	42,000	29,000	26,000
Total factory overhead	640,680	460,399	65,000	70,594
Selling expense	265,000	201,200	120,000	129,000
Payroll tax payable	26,500	20,120	12,000	12,900
Travel and transportation	35,620	10,613	26,000	29,000
Bad debt losses	80,000	75,000	40,000	47,800
Advertising	20,000	-0-	14,000	11,561
Total selling expense	427,120	306,933	212,000	230,261
Total cost of sales	2,271,200	3,069,330	3,402,000	3,696,000

Figure 11.1   Income statement with cost of sales schedule.

STATEMENT OF FINANCIAL CONDITION—12/30/78

	Hero Manufacturing		Rotten Distribution	
	Present Year 12/30/19X2	Previous Year 12/30/19X1	Present Year 12/30/19X2	Previous Year 12/30/19X1
Assets				
Current assets				
Cash	200,000	353,400	(5,000)	50,000
Securities	900,000	623,483	-0-	-0-
Accounts receivable	580,000	528,367	690,410	712,300
Allowance for uncollectables	(30,000)	(27,300)	(60,000)	(61,000)
Inventory	330,300	386,000	583,310	551,300
Prepaid expense	69,500	69,500	-0-	-0-
Total current assets	2,049,800	1,933,450	1,208,720	1,252,600
Fixed assets				
Furniture and fixtures	75,000	75,000	12,000	12,000
Equipment	520,500	303,503	195,000	195,000
Vehicles	90,000	85,000	55,000	45,000
Buildings and leasehold improvements	350,000	350,000	200,000	200,000
Less: Accumulated depreciation	(302,000)	(191,453)	(52,000)	(43,000)
Land	100,000	100,000	30,000	30,000
Total fixed assets	833,500	722,050	420,000	439,000
Other assets				
Investment in subsidiary	-0-	-0-	271,280	238,000
Organizational expense	40,000	40,000	50,000	50,000
Less: Amortization	(35,000)	(32,000)	(20,000)	(17,000)
Trademarks	-0-	-0-	40,000	40,000
Notes receivable from officers			200,000	178,000
Total other assets	5,000	8,000	541,280	489,000
Total assets	2,888,300	2,663,500	2,170,000	2,180,600

Liabilties

Current liabilities:				
Accounts payable	209,490	129,950	512,000	507,800
Payroll taxes payable	57,010	48,000	35,000	39,000
Provision for income tax	60,300	42,250	12,600	52,800
Notes payable	162,900	156,500	510,000	469,582
Accrued wages	10,062	10,000	10,062	9,518
Other accruals	-0-	153,400	11,458	10,000
Total current liabilities	499,762	543,700	1,091,120	1,088,700
Long-term liabilities				
Mortgages payable	320,338	331,000	160,000	173,000
Notes payable	339,000	285,000	218,880	208,300
Total long-term liabilities	659,338	616,000	378,880	281,300
Total liabilities	1,159,100	1,159,100	1,470,000	1,870,000
Net Worth:				
Common stock	300,000	30,000	810,600	801,400
Preferred stock	50,000	50,000	N/A	N/A
Paid-in surplus	150,000	150,000	N/A	N/A
Retained earnings	1,229,200	1,004,400	29,400	79,200
Less: Owner's draw	N/A	N/A	75,000	50,000
Principal debt repay	N/A	N/A	65,000	20,000
Total net worth	1,729,200	1,504,400	700,000	810,600
Total liabilities and net worth	2,888,300	2,663,500	2,170,000	2,180,600

Figure 11.2   Statement of financial condition.

Line of Business (and number of concerns reporting)	Current assets to current debt	Net profits on net sales	Net profits on tangible net worth	Net profits on net working capital	Net sales to tangible net worth	Net sales to net working capital	Collection period	Net sales to inventory	Fixed assets to tangible net worth	Current debt to tangible net worth	Total debt to tangible net worth	Inventory to net working capital	Current debt to inventory	Funded debts to net working capital
	Times	Per cent	Per cent	Per cent	Times	Times	Days	Times	Per cent	Per cent	Per cent	Per cent	Per cent	Per cent
3821–22 Instruments, Measuring & Controlling (53)	4.32	5.71	15.30	18.03	3.14	3.81	51	5.8	28.4	21.3	47.5	56.1	45.6	23.7
	2.83	4.00	9.26	11.80	2.29	3.05	64	4.1	40.4	44.3	90.3	74.1	89.6	38.1
	2.28	1.41	3.29	4.80	1.71	2.17	83	3.1	57.9	71.8	130.4	89.4	97.9	64.5
3321–22–23 Iron & Steel Foundries (56)	3.45	4.86	15.92	33.38	3.59	8.13	40	21.6	47.9	22.6	33.1	31.5	77.3	16.8
	2.37	3.19	9.38	15.40	2.71	5.38	48	10.3	63.4	30.7	50.8	63.1	115.4	39.2
	2.02	2.07	5.55	12.08	2.09	3.72	60	5.9	79.0	53.8	80.5	89.1	177.6	75.1
2253 Knit Outerwear Mills (56)	2.94	3.91	19.97	27.82	6.46	8.73	30	9.9	13.2	35.8	58.4	58.3	80.0	12.8
	2.01	2.87	11.71	16.33	4.04	6.40	49	6.9	28.4	60.6	89.0	96.8	114.9	33.8
	1.55	1.35	5.77	9.18	2.84	4.18	68	4.7	54.8	126.9	163.1	147.2	154.9	61.7
2082 Malt Liquors (30)	2.92	5.08	9.84	32.80	4.16	12.75	11	18.3	53.7	17.8	40.0	34.1	129.5	39.8
	2.31	1.65	4.97	12.64	2.49	8.95	16	15.1	70.7	24.9	58.2	55.6	137.4	94.4
	1.74	(0.55)	(1.61)	(6.23)	2.07	5.69	25	11.6	103.8	44.0	91.4	77.9	210.0	138.8
2515 Mattresses & Bedsprings (46)	3.36	3.03	12.24	15.35	6.05	8.18	41	11.3	14.4	24.6	65.6	55.8	65.8	13.0
	2.58	1.38	5.12	9.18	3.78	5.70	50	7.7	29.1	46.2	95.2	76.7	101.1	38.9
	1.69	0.55	3.39	4.17	2.36	4.00	61	6.4	50.0	92.3	131.8	103.9	140.8	76.5
2011 Meat Packing Plants (92)	3.70	1.33	14.79	25.89	19.05	34.13	12	21.6	42.9	23.9	58.2	34.1	87.3	16.5
	2.00	0.67	8.57	17.96	10.45	19.79	15	30.1	63.2	52.7	95.9	69.0	143.3	47.6
	1.47	0.20	2.59	5.73	7.00	12.57	20	21.2	90.0	100.6	184.5	111.4	227.7	88.4
3461 Metal Stampings (104)	4.35	4.90	12.16	21.75	4.39	8.16	34	11.1	30.9	17.4	44.0	44.4	64.5	26.4
	2.55	2.84	7.93	13.33	3.11	5.06	43	7.3	54.1	34.6	71.8	71.6	105.7	59.2
	1.67	0.72	2.59	6.22	1.94	3.48	58	5.2	82.2	72.0	153.5	102.4	162.4	85.6
3541–42–44–45–48 Metalworking Machinery & Equipment (124)	4.36	5.93	12.76	20.02	3.23	5.54	46	13.4	34.8	18.9	38.8	36.2	56.4	15.0
	2.83	3.06	6.94	11.21	2.13	3.46	61	5.9	48.3	29.8	71.4	66.2	91.1	43.1
	1.96	0.62	0.93	1.75	1.49	2.29	76	3.2	69.6	62.0	114.8	92.5	161.0	76.8
2431 Millwork (55)	4.14	4.25	21.08	29.04	6.25	8.56	34	10.9	23.7	26.0	58.9	52.6	72.0	17.1
	2.27	2.61	10.08	16.83	4.10	5.74	48	8.1	39.0	51.3	106.0	73.9	94.5	44.7
	1.75	1.37	5.40	6.08	2.92	4.09	59	5.5	61.8	87.8	204.9	118.2	144.6	77.7
3599 Miscellanous Machinery, except Electrical (90)	4.45	5.75	14.65	28.54	4.03	7.14	33	23.8	32.7	19.0	29.7	22.5	61.8	7.9
	2.71	3.20	6.87	12.70	2.76	4.67	46	9.4	51.1	32.8	59.1	54.2	103.1	27.5
	1.84	1.23	3.89	7.49	1.83	3.44	61	5.0	70.8	65.4	113.3	87.3	194.7	70.1
3714 Motor Vehicle Parts & Accessories (89)	3.70	5.72	16.23	26.74	3.60	5.91	35	9.0	27.2	25.6	55.2	55.2	54.8	27.8
	2.77	4.26	11.53	19.20	2.68	3.93	44	5.8	44.3	37.1	78.4	73.3	80.3	47.4
	2.19	2.96	8.22	11.21	2.16	2.87	54	4.1	62.5	55.4	117.9	96.0	116.7	73.1
3361–62–69 Nonferrous Foundries (47)	4.03	5.65	14.63	29.96	4.05	8.71	42	18.9	33.3	18.6	34.2	27.6	74.2	12.9
	2.75	2.74	8.63	17.46	3.01	5.28	47	13.4	54.5	29.1	84.9	44.5	130.4	30.0
	1.59	1.08	1.41	5.79	2.15	4.00	53	6.7	77.8	73.6	175.3	83.7	260.4	122.5
2541–42 Office & Store Fixtures (60)	3.54	5.66	16.00	26.81	4.80	9.50	36	12.2	20.2	30.8	79.2	45.1	74.6	25.4
	2.22	2.45	8.58	12.85	3.52	4.86	50	7.7	42.8	55.8	114.3	75.8	116.4	46.9
	1.59	0.48	2.21	2.34	2.23	3.32	70	4.5	70.6	91.2	155.5	123.7	174.4	109.0
2361–63–69 Outerwear, Children's & Infants' (58)	2.70	2.46	15.29	18.50	8.83	12.11	30	12.9	6.8	46.9	55.7	51.1	81.1	7.4
	1.89	1.40	8.31	10.18	5.80	7.84	42	7.5	11.2	92.1	116.9	89.9	126.8	18.7
	1.46	0.49	2.54	2.72	3.69	4.50	60	5.9	24.2	175.5	315.8	146.5	208.7	37.5
2851 Paints, Varnishes, Lacquers & Enamels (112)	3.81	3.96	12.91	20.55	4.60	6.80	35	8.7	25.4	23.3	44.4	58.1	53.3	15.6
	2.92	2.61	8.87	13.50	3.40	4.85	46	6.4	40.8	40.1	72.6	73.3	81.3	33.1
	2.13	1.50	5.39	6.87	2.51	3.43	59	5.5	55.4	64.2	106.8	89.3	109.7	56.1
2621 Paper Mills, except Building Paper (55)	3.52	4.91	10.01	28.19	2.56	6.22	34	11.4	67.8	19.0	50.5	46.7	68.0	39.9
	2.82	3.28	6.27	14.02	1.97	4.30	43	7.8	87.4	22.1	75.4	60.6	98.0	117.4
	2.17	1.56	3.27	6.85	1.67	3.78	54	6.2	117.5	40.5	121.4	82.7	172.3	156.7
2651–52–53–54–55 Paperboard Containers & Boxes (61)	4.17	3.87	19.66	30.20	4.37	10.80	33	11.7	46.7	17.1	59.1	54.3	64.4	40.3
	2.22	2.63	7.38	14.20	3.06	6.45	36	8.0	70.5	38.3	75.2	80.0	92.8	67.5
	1.64	1.35	4.28	7.95	2.06	4.76	44	6.2	101.2	64.1	129.1	140.9	162.7	124.5
3712–13 Passenger Car, Truck & Bus Bodies (46)	3.54	3.14	14.02	19.64	6.78	7.67	29	9.0	18.5	25.6	47.6	59.4	64.1	17.3
	2.07	1.82	8.48	10.11	4.21	5.35	41	8.1	30.5	69.2	116.0	88.6	90.8	31.9
	1.49	1.16	4.21	6.14	2.46	3.92	56	4.3	66.3	128.5	218.6	141.1	151.9	48.1

( ) Indicates Loss

Figure 11.3. Dun and Bradstreet, *Key Business Ratios: Manufacturing and Construction.* Courtesy of Dun and Bradstreet, Inc.

small a profit margin may indicate ineffective management or other internal problems. Every company has as its goal the maximum realization of profit from each dollar of sales. This ratio measures a company's success in achieving that goal. The net profit to sales ratio is calculated by dividing the net profit after taxes by the net (after returns and allowances) sales:

$$\text{net profit on net sales} = \frac{\text{net profit after tax}}{\text{net sales}}$$

Example.   Hero Manufacturing   Rotten Distribution

$$\frac{\$\ 224,800}{5,620,000} = 4.0\% \qquad \frac{\$\ 29,400}{4,200,000} = 0.7\%$$

Four percent of Hero Mfg.'s sales go to profit after tax, whereas Rotten Dist. is making about a half of a percent, 0.7%, net profit margin. For Hero, the industry average is 3.19% and the best in the industry is 4.85%. Hero is better than the

Line of Business (and number of concerns reporting)	Current assets to current debt (Times)	Net profits on net sales (Per cent)	Net profits on tangible net worth (Per cent)	Net profits on net working capital (Per cent)	Net sales to tangible net worth (Times)	Net sales to net working capital (Times)	Collection period (Days)	Net sales to inventory (Times)	Fixed assets to tangible net worth (Per cent)	Current debt to tangible net worth (Per cent)	Total debt to tangible net worth (Per cent)	Inventory to net working capital (Per cent)	Current debt to inventory (Per cent)	Funded debt to net working capital (Per cent)
5097 Furniture & Home Furnishings (81)	2.98	3.40	14.42	20.14	6.85	7.82	40	9.5	6.8	42.3	74.1	58.0	66.6	16.0
	2.10	1.58	8.42	10.08	4.83	5.50	49	6.8	13.5	75.4	140.2	88.1	108.7	31.7
	1.67	0.94	4.17	5.94	3.24	4.33	70	4.6	30.7	138.3	198.4	117.8	138.3	43.9
5041 Groceries, General Line (196)	3.15	1.21	13.86	16.81	20.27	25.58	8	18.0	11.7	39.7	83.1	86.8	49.7	20.9
	2.00	0.57	7.77	9.70	12.43	15.08	12	12.5	32.3	80.2	136.1	123.0	76.8	37.4
	1.51	0.23	3.49	4.30	7.69	9.45	17	8.7	67.7	139.7	224.8	172.8	108.6	83.2
5072 Hardware (174)	4.08	2.62	10.81	13.08	5.71	7.20	32	6.6	6.3	26.3	55.5	75.2	38.4	6.5
	2.82	1.76	7.02	8.34	3.80	4.61	43	4.9	13.6	50.9	90.7	97.1	67.0	19.8
	1.81	0.80	3.64	4.07	2.73	3.31	52	3.7	25.1	98.2	152.9	130.0	100.6	36.2
5084 Industrial Machinery & Equipment (97)	3.27	3.78	17.24	23.65	7.90	8.80	34	11.2	8.4	35.5	79.6	62.5	65.4	13.5
	2.12	2.03	8.50	11.83	4.73	5.50	43	6.6	18.8	88.5	134.0	92.1	103.0	41.7
	1.59	0.75	4.17	4.76	3.24	4.04	59	4.0	46.6	139.7	216.8	125.1	150.3	67.9
5098 Lumber & Construction Materials (146)	3.60	3.05	16.67	23.17	8.64	11.36	36	11.3	8.8	32.5	75.3	52.5	60.3	14.0
	2.20	1.85	11.00	13.02	5.73	6.18	47	8.0	21.0	88.5	129.0	83.7	104.4	33.8
	1.64	0.94	6.18	7.00	3.38	4.01	64	5.8	39.5	124.6	247.4	118.4	173.2	64.7
5047 Meats & Meat Products (48)	2.93	1.33	21.62	22.58	25.38	29.41	15	76.4	9.6	37.2	65.9	33.5	133.5	12.8
	2.03	0.74	12.13	13.75	16.94	20.44	22	42.0	29.0	79.2	114.5	50.3	197.1	36.7
	1.45	0.23	3.54	4.72	9.36	14.67	30	24.2	50.0	175.3	256.6	104.1	378.0	71.3
5091 Metals & Minerals (76)	4.03	3.54	14.13	21.01	6.34	7.46	39	7.9	11.2	28.9	54.1	57.8	54.1	11.5
	2.36	2.07	8.44	10.51	4.04	4.96	47	5.3	22.2	66.2	110.5	83.3	85.9	27.3
	1.51	1.21	5.11	6.57	2.38	3.45	60	3.7	43.5	134.7	172.7	141.1	130.5	59.4
5028 Paints & Varnishes (38)	6.13	3.56	12.92	19.35	4.74	6.29	33	8.0	6.1	17.7	33.8	45.0	42.4	7.0
	3.50	2.55	5.52	8.09	3.29	4.26	41	6.4	16.1	25.6	68.1	68.4	68.4	16.1
	2.00	1.13	3.10	4.76	2.52	3.27	48	5.4	27.7	70.9	93.7	93.0	99.9	40.3
5096 Paper & Its Products (121)	3.88	2.33	11.31	14.92	8.06	10.73	31	11.8	7.8	30.4	67.6	57.1	57.5	12.2
	2.34	1.23	7.00	8.79	5.39	6.66	40	8.1	14.5	59.8	107.4	83.2	95.9	23.1
	1.70	0.60	3.43	4.26	3.63	4.61	51	6.1	35.7	104.2	177.6	102.2	146.6	53.8
5092 Petroleum & Petroleum Products (66)	3.45	3.21	14.52	37.55	7.70	15.38	25	35.4	26.6	20.7	42.3	23.1	112.7	18.9
	2.07	1.31	9.09	16.02	4.80	9.40	34	24.2	48.5	38.8	90.3	47.9	174.0	62.3
	1.50	0.69	3.53	8.79	3.08	5.59	52	13.7	86.7	86.5	189.1	84.3	287.5	130.0
5033 Piece Goods (128)	3.17	2.39	11.04	13.84	8.13	8.91	29	9.1	2.1	43.9	61.1	62.5	59.4	8.7
	2.10	1.36	6.35	7.22	4.74	5.96	47	6.1	5.0	84.1	122.2	91.2	100.8	17.4
	1.64	0.67	3.68	3.89	3.25	3.51	68	4.6	15.2	132.8	176.8	124.3	146.5	41.2
5074 Plumbing & Heating Equipment & Supplies (179)	3.66	3.13	13.04	16.30	6.58	7.62	36	8.4	6.8	31.4	59.8	65.4	53.0	9.8
	2.83	1.77	7.76	9.72	4.50	5.24	45	6.0	13.2	53.3	97.9	82.5	79.9	20.4
	1.94	0.99	4.28	5.39	3.32	3.70	58	4.8	28.4	99.2	158.6	106.1	120.0	44.1
5044 Poultry & Poultry Products (45)	3.39	2.21	15.79	31.97	14.44	25.90	14	66.7	12.1	27.1	61.0	24.7	111.9	19.4
	2.08	0.83	8.11	10.77	10.52	16.16	21	31.1	26.5	59.3	104.2	48.4	157.8	95.4
	1.39	0.26	2.55	3.50	6.47	8.17	31	15.0	80.8	108.7	263.0	100.0	248.2	187.0
5093 Scrap & Waste Materials (61)	4.10	3.37	12.11	24.18	7.32	10.61	20	30.0	19.3	21.3	36.3	28.5	50.1	15.9
	2.41	1.80	6.86	12.37	3.74	7.91	30	11.5	38.0	37.2	103.1	60.0	137.3	47.8
	1.54	0.80	4.72	8.09	2.67	4.39	48	7.1	59.4	88.3	182.8	103.6	229.5	107.7
5014 Tires & Tubes (44)	2.58	3.09	14.15	17.50	6.11	8.26	32	9.7	13.8	50.1	101.2	60.7	84.6	8.9
	1.93	1.80	7.69	10.00	4.51	5.87	42	6.0	24.9	87.3	122.3	94.0	118.7	30.4
	1.58	0.93	3.67	6.21	3.43	4.33	63	4.4	45.1	125.7	251.6	137.0	150.0	66.7
5094 Tobacco & Its Products (97)	2.71	1.04	13.94	23.78	21.35	27.49	13	25.6	9.4	46.2	81.0	60.7	81.2	8.8
	1.97	0.73	9.85	13.12	12.40	17.28	18	18.5	17.3	82.5	118.2	93.0	114.1	20.9
	1.43	0.40	5.40	7.02	7.48	10.42	24	12.3	31.9	152.0	170.1	141.5	164.0	40.9

Figure 11.4.   Dun and Bradstreet, *Key Business Ratios: Wholesaling.* Courtesy of Dun and Bradstreet, Inc.

industry average, and almost as good as the best. Rotten's industry average is 1.59%, and the worst is 0.8%. Rotten does worse than the worst.

Fixed Assets to Tangible Net Worth.   This ratio indicates what percentage of your company's net worth is invested in fixed assets. Ordinarily, this ratio should not exceed 100% for a manufacturer, and 75% for a wholesaler or retailer; but industries differ widely on this ratio, and it is necessary to check the industry ratio. A percentage beyond the maximum limits of the industry indicates that a disproportionate amount of capital is frozen in machinery and the building itself. This will limit the amount of operating funds for carrying inventories, receivables, and maintaining day-to-day cash outlays. It also means that the business will be unprepared for the hazards of unexpected developments (and every business gets its share of those) and drains income into heavy debt payment and maintenance charges. But remember, a high percentage for this ratio does not automatically prove that fixed assets are excessive. The ratio may be distorted by inadequate net worth or recent investment in modernizing an out of date plant.

The fixed assets to tangible net worth ratio is computed by dividing fixed assets by net worth and is expressed as a percentage:

$$\text{fixed assets to tangible net worth} = \frac{\text{total fixed assets}}{\text{tangible net worth}}$$

Example.

Hero Manufacturing	Rotten Distribution

$$\frac{\$\ 833,500}{1,724,200} = 48.3\% \qquad \frac{\$420,000}{630,000} = 66.7\%$$

Hero Manufacturing does not have excessive fixed assets. Fixed assets are a smaller percentage of net worth than the industry average (63.4%). Rotten's fixed assets are much too large a percentage of net worth, a higher percentage than the industry average (37.2) and almost the industry worst (88.3). This indicates that Rotten has too many—and probably unproductive—fixed assets, which limits the amount they have for day-to-day operations.

Financial Management Ratios

Financial management ratios are a general group of ratios which are perhaps the most widely used in finance. Financial lenders such as banks and private sources will generally compute the current asset to current liability ratio and the debt to net worth ratio as a first step to evaluating any business.

These ratios give the general financial picture of a business, including its debt load, how well owner's equity is providing returns from inventories, how sales are doing in relation to the money invested in the business, and so on.

These ratios show general financial performance and trends for each business. It is good for the businessperson to remember that these ratios are almost always calculated when financing is sought from outside (banks, bonding, etc.). Therefore, it would be wise to calculate these ratios *before* going to a lender, to see if your company is strong enough or if it might have some problems securing loans.

Current Ratio (Current Assets to Current Liabilities). The current ratio measures a company's liquidity and the extent of protection for short-term creditors. It gives a general picture of the adequacy of the company's working capital and its ability to meet day-to-day payment obligations. It measures the margin of safety provided for paying current debts in the event of a reduction in the value of current assets. If receivables and inventory are valid, the current ratio is important as a specific measure of the capacity of a company to meet daily financing requirements.

To calculate the ratio, divide the total current assets by the total current liabilities as follows:

$$\text{current ratio} = \frac{\text{total current assets}}{\text{total current liabilities}}$$

Example.

Hero Manufacturing	Rotten Distribution

$$\frac{\$2,049,800}{499,762} = 4.1 \text{ times} \qquad \frac{\$1,208,720}{1,091,120} = 1.11 \text{ times}$$

In the example, Hero Manufacturing has enough current assets to cover its current liabilities approximately four times. If it was forced to liquidate its current assets to pay its current liabilities it would have much more than it needed to pay off obligations. If you look at the industry ratios for iron and steel foundries (Figure 11.3), you can see that the lowest times assets cover liabilities is 2.02; the average 2.37 times; and the highest 3.45 times. With a ratio of 4.1 times Hero is not only above the industry average, it is higher than the highest ratio recorded for the industry.

Rotten Distribution, on the other hand, had a very poor ratio. With only 1.11 times coverage, if nip comes to tuck it would barely be able to cover current liabilities with the liquidation of current assets. Rotten has a ratio that is lower than the lowest in the industry, just the opposite of Hero. For the scrap and waste materials wholesale industry (Figure 11.4), the highest current ratio is 4.1 times; average, 2.41 times; and lowest, 1.54 times.

Current Debt to Tangible Net Worth.   This ratio is infrequently used. (The more frequently used ratio, total liabilities (total debt) to net worth, follows). This ratio of current debt to worth should not exceed 80%, and generally the higher the percentage, the more the company depends on current financing to meet operation capital requirements. The current debt to tangible net worth ratio is computed by dividing current liabilities by tangible net worth and is expressed as a percentage:

$$\text{current debt to tangible net worth} = \frac{\text{current liabilities}}{\text{tangible net worth}}$$

Example.

Hero Manufacturing   Rotten Distribution

$$\frac{\$\ 499,762}{1,724,200} = 29\% \qquad \frac{\$1,091,120}{630,000} = 173.4\%$$

Hero Manufacturing has current liabilities as a percentage of tangible net worth at pretty close to the industry average (30.7%), which indicates that it uses current liabilities no more than the industry in general. Rotten Distribution is very dependent on short-term (current liability) financing. As a matter of fact, it is more dependent on current liability financing than anyone in the industry (highest percentage: 88.3%).

Net Sales to Tangible Net Worth.   The net sales to net worth ratio is sometimes known as the trading ratio. It indiciates that the extent to which a company's sales volume is supported by invested capital (net worth). A substantially higher than average ratio indicates that the company is an overtrader, that is, a company that is attempting to stretch the invested dollar to its maximum capacity. The overtrader's financial statement shows heavy debt. When a business has heavy debt its survival will hinge on the long-term continuation of optimum internal and external conditions. The undertrader, on the other hand, has either large capital reserves or inadequate sales to support the business. The most pressing need of the undertrader is generally to bring sales up to a profitable level. The net sales to net worth ratio measures the degree to which a company has attained a balance between the extremes of undertrading and overtrading.

In other words, the ratio is a measure of the relative turnover of capital. If capital is turned over too rapidly, liabilities build up excessively. If capital is turned too slowly, funds become stagnant and profitability suffers. The net sales to net worth ratio is calculated as net sales divided by tangible net worth (net worth minus intangibles):

$$\text{net sales to tangible net worth} = \frac{\text{net sales}}{\text{tangible net worth}}$$

Example.

Hero Manufacturing	Rotten Distribution
$\dfrac{\$5,620,000}{1,724,200} = 3.25 \text{ times}$	$\dfrac{\$4,200,000}{630,000} = 6.67 \text{ times}$

Hero Manufacturing turned its capital over a little more than the industry average of 2.71 times. Yet it can not be considered as overtrading because it came in well below the industry's greatest overtraders, who turned capital 3.59 times. A quick look at Hero's large cash and security amounts and at the current ratio indicates that it has more than enough working capital to pay any foreseeable short-term obligation. Rotten Distribution turns its capital over twice as much as Hero, but still has to go some distance before it can equal the worst in the industry at 7.32 times. The industry average is 3.74 times, higher than the average in Hero's industry.

Net Sales to Net Working Capital.   This ratio indicates the demands made upon working capital to support the sales volume of the company. It is much like the ratio above except that it measures the turnover of working capital. If the ratio is too high, there is a tendency of the business to owe too much money. Turning working capital very fast necessitates dependence upon credit granted by suppliers, banks and others to provide operating funds. In cases where this ratio is disproportionately high, there is a good indication of working capital deficiencies.

The net sales to net working capital ratio is calculated by dividing net sales by net working capital:

$$\text{net sales to working capital} = \frac{\text{net sales}}{\text{working capital}}$$

Example.

Hero Manufacturing	Rotten Distribution
$\dfrac{\$5,620,000}{1,550,000} = 3.63 \text{ times}$	$\dfrac{\$4,200,000}{117,600} = 35.7 \text{ times}$

Hero Manufacturing obviously has plenty of working capital because it turns so slowly. As a matter of fact, Hero turns its working capital slower than the best in the industry (3.72 times); the industry average is 5.3 times. Rotten Distribution is 180 degrees in the opposite direction. Rotten turns its working capital over three times faster than the worst in its industry (10.61 times). Rotten turns its working capital five times more than the industry average (7.51 times).

Net Profit on Tangible Net Worth.   This ratio measures the return on invested capital and gauges the possibilities of future growth. The tendency today is to look more and more to this ratio, rather than to the profit to sales ratio above, as a criterion of profitability. Generally, a profits to worth relationship of at least 10% is regarded as necessary for providing draw or dividends plus funds for future growth. Tangible net worth is net worth *minus* such intangibles as goodwill, patents, copyrights, trademarks, organization expense, and treasury stock. To arrive at Hero Manufacturing's tangible net worth we have to subtract $5000 amortized value of the organization expense from $1,729,200 net worth, leaving $1,724,200. In the case of Rotten Distribution, we must subtract $40,000 in trademarks, and $30,000 amortized value of organization expense from a net worth of $700,000, leaving $620,000. The net profit to net worth is calculated by dividing net profit by net worth:

$$\text{net profit to net worth} = \frac{\text{net profit after tax}}{\text{tangible net worth}}$$

Example.

Hero Manufacturing	Rotten Distribution
$\frac{\$224,800}{1,724,200} = 13.0\%$	$\frac{\$29,400}{630,000} = 4.67\%$

Hero Manufacturing is returning 13% on net worth (investment) to its owners. This is a good return for the industry, better than the average return of 9.39%, and almost as good as the top industry return of 15.92%. Rotten Distribution's return to its owners isn't as good as the industry average of 6.95% (the scrap industry has a lower average return than the iron and steel foundries). Rotten (again) did worse than the worse company recorded at 4.72%. How does Rotten Distribution survive!

Total Debt (Total Liabilities) to Tangible Net Worth.   Sometimes simply called the debt to worth ratio, this ratio measures the proportion of the owner's investment in the business compared to the creditors' investment. If the total debt exceeds the net worth, it means that the suppliers and the banks have invested more than the owner. The management of top-heavy liabilities entails strains and hazards that can become a threat to business survival. They expose the business to unexpected risks such as a sudden downturn in sales, changes in customer preferences; strikes, fires, rapid rises in business costs, and other factors. Companies that have a lower than average ratio indicate a strong ownership interest. On the other hand, long-term debt has its own peril in that it is generally more exactly fixed as to maturity and more enforceable because almost all long-term debt is supported by specifically pledged collateral.

The total debt to tangible net worth ratio is calculated by dividing total liabilities by tangible net worth, expressed as a percentage:

$$\text{total debt to tangible net worth} = \frac{\text{total liabilities}}{\text{tangible net worth}}$$

Example.

Hero Manufacturing	Rotten Distribution
$\frac{\$1,470,000}{1,724,200} = 85.3\%$	$\frac{\$1,470,000}{630,000} = 233\%$

Hero Manufacturing has a weak percentage of total liabilities compared to the net worth, though more than the industry percentage (58.8%). Hero's percentage is also slightly more than the highest in the industry (80%). Rotten Distribution exceeds the worst percentage in its industry (182.8%) which again points up Rotten's strong dependence on outside financing to the tune of twice its net worth.

MANAGING INVESTMENTS IN ASSETS

The owner of a business may have the best of financial records. They may be presented in the right form at the right time. But if he or she has not learned how to use the information, it will be of little value. Skill in financial management—like skill in shop practice, selling, or any other business activity—comes from experience. That experience, however, must be built upon knowledge and understanding of some fundamental principles.

Sound financial management is essentially sound asset management, and one of the most important aspects of asset management is close control of your investment in two areas: fixed assets and receivables.

Care should be taken that the investment in each of these assets is not larger than you really need, considering the type of business you are in and the requirements and goals of your company. More specific guides are described in the following paragraphs.

Investment in Fixed Assets

Holding down your investment in fixed assets is important for these reasons:

1. If too much of your capital is tied up in fixed assets, you may have too little left for working capital.
2. Investments in fixed assets typically last for a long time. They may be difficult and costly to reconvert into cash if changed circumstances or plans should make this necessary.
3. Fixed charges resulting from a high investment in fixed assets may become a heavy burden during periods of low sales or falling prices. These fixed charges include interest on long-term debt, insurance on plant and equipment, taxes, and maintenance charges.
4. Heavy fixed costs growing out of overinvestment in fixed assets raise the break-even point.

How Much is Too Much?   There is no specific answer to this question. Some businesses must, because of their nature, have relatively heavy investments in fixed assets. If these businesses are to earn a satisfactory return on investment, they must have a high profit margin and/or a large proportion of low-cost debt money to finance fixed assets.

One measure you can use in judging your company's asset investment is the proportion of your total assets represented by fixed assets (fixed assets divided by total assets). Like other ratios, this one should be compared with the performance of companies similar to yours or with your own figures for earlier periods.

Another useful measure is the turnover of fixed assets (net sales divided by net fixed assets), which tells you how many dollars' worth of goods or services were sold for each dollar invested in fixed assets.

What Can You Do About It?   There are several steps you can take to hold down your investment in fixed assets.

Mortgaging fixed assets makes it possible to use buildings and equipment with a minimum investment. Financing is available on liberal credit terms for most types of new machines. And while loans on building are not always as easy to get as equipment financing, you may be able to borrow a substantial part of the purchase price if the building is modern and of standard design. Some industrial foundations and state and municipal financing agencies occasionally sell new buildings with no down payment.

Leasing is another way to avoid high investment in fixed assets. Almost all types of fixed assets can be leased—trucks, office furniture, equipment, machinery, buildings, land, and so on. In fact, a business can sometimes release capital by selling assets and leasing them back from the purchaser.

Care should be used, however, in entering into lease and mortgage agreements, especially if the prospects of the business are uncertain. Such commitments, like borrowing, bring fixed charges that must be paid on schedule regardless of business conditions.

Subcontracting production lessens the need for investment in fixed assets and also the expense involved in care and maintenance.

Investment in Receivables

The size of your investment in accounts receivable depends on a number of factors:

1. The volume of credit sales (the most important factor).
2. Your credit terms.
3. The payment practices of your customers.
4. The firmness with which you collect overdue accounts.

For instance, you may decide to offer more lenient credit terms or to extend credit to a few somewhat "risky" customers in order to increase sales. This will tend to increase the volume of receivables.

Or, you may wish to change your credit terms so as to shorten the collection period (remember, however, that this type of change may reduce sales revenues). You might, for example, substitute terms calling for payment 30 days from the date of sale instead of 30 days after the end of the month in which the sale was made. Discounts for early payment might be allowed or increased. These steps will tend to decrease the volume of receivables.

Once you have established your credit terms and collection practices, the level of receivables can be expected to vary directly with sales volume. If it does not, a change in the pattern of payments has taken place, and you should inquire into the reasons for the change.

Keeping an Eye on Receivables.   The average collection period (explained earlier) enables you to compare your collection record with the credit terms you offer. Over time, it also shows up changes in the pattern of payments.

Another very important technique for keeping track of your receivables investment is the aging schedule. In an aging schedule, the accounts receivable are classified according to date of sale and summarized as in the following example:

Receivables outstanding as of 12/31/19XX	Amount	Percent
Receivables outstanding less than 30 days	$22,610	70
Receivables outstanding 30 to 45 days	3,530	11
Receivables outstanding 45 to 60 days	3,510	11
Receivables outstanding 60 to 90 days	1,910	6
Receivables oustanding 90 days or more	620	2
Total	$32,180	100

The aging schedule shows to what extent old accounts are piling up. It suggests which accounts and what proportions of accounts need special attention if sizable bad debt losses are to be avoided. In addition to being a valuable management tool, it is often required by bankers and other lenders.

Lazarus Time sat in his car after class looking out at the night sky. "Well," he thought, "it has been several weeks since I first decided to get into this accounting thing. I've taken classes, read articles, kept actual books, and talked to a Certified Public Accountant. All this to get a loan." Now the class was over and the company still needed money. Lazarus wondered if he had really learned anything.

He did know one thing—before he went for another loan, he was going to do all the ratios on his business, check them against the industry averages, and at least know as much as the banker Mr. Pumiceheart knew.

Lazarus could see the limousine in front of the class building. As usual, it was waiting to pick up the instructor. Lazarus watched the limo. A beautiful lady got out of the back. Lazarus looked closely—it was Suzi Wo, the lady he had talked to in class.

The instructor came out the door. Suzi moved slowly to the instructor and kissed him. The instructor climbed into the limo.

"At least he got something out of accounting," Lazarus thought as the limo with the rich and beautiful lady whisked the professor away into the night.

Glossary

Accelerated depreciation. A method of depreciation that charges off more of the original cost of the fixed assets in the earlier years than in the later years of the asset's service life.

Account. A recording unit used to reflect the changes in assets, liabilities or owners' equity.

Account receivable. An amount that is owed to the business, usually by one of its customers, as a result of the ordinary extension of credit.

Accounting period. The period of time over which an income statement summarizes the changes in owners' equity; usually, the period is one year.

Accrual basis. The measurement of revenues and expenses, as contrasted with receipts and expenditures.

Accrued expense. A liability arising because an expense occurs in a period prior to the related expenditure.

Accumulated depreciation. An account showing the total amount of depreciation of an asset that has been accumulated to date.

Acid-test ratio. The ratio obtained by dividing quick assets by current liabilities.

Allowance for doubtful accounts. The amount of estimated bad debts that is subtracted from accounts receivable on the balance sheet.

Amortization. The process of writing off the cost of intangible assets; similar to depreciation.

Asset. An item which is owned by the business and has a value that can be measured objectively.

Auditing. A review of accounting records by independent, outside public accountants.

Bad debts. The estimated amount of credit sales that will not be collected.

Balance. The difference between the totals of the two sides of an account.

Balance sheet. A financial statement which reports the assets and equities of a company at one point in time. Assets are listed on the left and equities on the right.

Bond. A written promise to repay money furnished to the business, with interest, at some future date, usually five or more years hence.

Capital stock. A balance sheet account showing the amount that was assigned to the shares of stock at the time they were originally issued.

Capital turnover. A ratio obtained by dividing annual sales by investment.

Cash basis accounting. An accounting system that does not use the accrual basis.

Closing. The transfer of the balance from one account to another account.

Common stock. Stock whose owners are not entitled to preferential treatment with regard to dividends or to the distribution of assets in the event of liquidation; usually, common stockholders control the company.

Cost accounting. The process of identifying manufacturing costs and assigning them to inventory in the manufacturing process.

Cost concept. Assets are ordinarily valued at the price paid to acquire them.

Cost of goods sold. The cost of the merchandise sold to customers.

Credit. The right-hand side of an account or an amount entered on the right-hand side of an account.

Creditor. A person who lends money or extends credit to a business.

Current assets. Assets which are either currently in the form of cash or are expected to be converted into cash within a short period of time; usually one year.

Current liabilities. Obligations which become due within a short period of time usually one year.

Current ratio. The ratio obtained by dividing the total of the current assets by the total of the current liabilities.

Days' receivables. The number of days of sales that are tied up in accounts receivable.

Debt. The left-hand side of an account, or an amount entered on the left-hand side of an account.

Debt capital. The capital raised by the issuance of bonds.

Debt ratio. The ratio obtained by dividing debt capital by total capital.

Deferred revenue. The liability that arises when a customer pays a business in advance for a service or product. It is a liability because the business has an obligation to render the service or deliver the product.

Depletion. The process of writing off the cost of a wasting asset.

Depreciation. The process of recognizing a portion of the cost of an asset as an expense during each year of its estimated service life.

Direct labor or material. The labor or material that is used directly on a product.

Dividend. The funds generated by profitable operations that are distributed to the shareholders.

Double-declining balance method. An accelerated method of depreciation.

Double-entry system. A characteristic of accounting in which each transaction recorded causes at least two changes in the accounts.

Dual aspect concept. The accounting concept which assumes that the total assets of a company always equal the total equities.

Earnings. Another term for net income.

Earnings per share. A ratio obtained by dividing the total earnings for a given period by the number of shares of common stock outstanding.

Entity concept. The accounting concept which assumes that accounts are kept for business entities, rather than for the persons who own, operate, or are otherwise associated with the business.

Entry. The accounting record made for a single transaction.

Equities. Claims against assets that are held by owners or by creditors.

Equity capital. The capital raised from owners.

Expenditure. An amount arising from the acquisition of an asset.

Expense. A decrease in owners' equity resulting from operations.

FIFO. The first-in, first-out inventory method which assumes that the goods that enter the inventory first are the first to be sold.

Fixed assets. The tangible properties of relatively long life that are generally used in the production of goods and services, rather than being held for resale.

Going-concern concept. The accounting concept which assumes that a business will continue to operate indefinitely.

Goodwill. An intangible asset; an amount paid for a favorable location or reputation.

Gross margin. The difference between sales revenue and cost of goods sold.

Income statement. A statement of revenues and expenses for a given period.

Interim statements. Financial statements prepared for a period of less than one year.

Inventories. Goods being held for sale, and material and partially finished products which will be sold upon completion.

Inventory turnover. Tells how many times inventory was totally replaced during the year; calculated by dividing the average inventory into costof goods sold.

Investments. Securities that are held for a relatively long period of time and are purchased for reasons other than the temporary use of excess cash. They are noncurrent assets.

Journal. A record in which entries are recorded in chronological order.

Lease. An agreement under which the owner of property permits someone else to use it.

Ledger. A group of accounts.

Liability. The equity or claim of a creditor.

LIFO. The last-in, first-out inventory method which assumes that the last goods purchased are the first to be sold.

Liquid assets. Cash and assets which are easily converted into cash.

Liquidity ratios. The relationship of obligations soon coming due to assets which should provide the cash for meeting these obligations.

Manufacturing overhead. All manufacturing costs that are not direct material or direct labor.

Market value. The amount for which an asset can be sold in the marketplace.

Marketable securities. Securities that are expected to be converted into cash within a year; a current asset.

Matching concept. Costs are matched against the revenue of a period.

Materiality concept. Disregard trivial matters; disclose all important matters.

Money measurement concept. A concept that assumes that Accounting records show only facts that can be expressed in monetary terms.

Mortgage. A pledge of real estate as security for a loan.

Net book value. The difference between the cost of a fixed asset and its accumulated depreciation.

Net income. The amount by which total revenues exceed total expenses for a given period.

Net loss. The amount by which total expenses exceed total revenues for a given period.

Nominal account. An income statement account that is closed at the end of the period to a balance sheet account.

Noncurrent liability. A claim which does not fall due within one year.

Note receivable. An amount owed that is evidenced by a promissory note.

Obsolescence. A loss in the usefulness of an asset because of the development of improved equipment, changes in style, or other causes not related to the physical condition of the asset.

Operating expenses. Costs associated with sales and administrative activities as distinct from those associated with production of goods or services.

Overhead rate. A rate used to allocate overhead costs to products.

Owners' equity. The claims of owners against the assets of a business.

Paid in capital. An amount in excess of the par or stated value of stock that is paid by investors.

Par value. The specific amount printed on the face of a stock certificate.

Partnership. An unincorporated business with two or more owners.

Period costs. Costs associated with general sales and administrative activities.

Permanent capital. Debt and equity capital.

Perpetual inventory. An individual record of the cost of each item in inventory.

Physical inventory. The counting of all merchandise currently on hand.

Posting. The process of transferring transactions from the journal to the ledger.

Preferred stock. Stock whose owners receive preferential treatment with regard to dividends or with regard to the distribution of assets in the event of liquidation.

Prepaid expenses. Services and certain intangibles purchased prior to the period during which their benefits are received; treated as assets until they are consumed.

Price-earnings ratio. A ratio obtained by dividing the average market price of the stock by the earnings per share.

Product costs. Costs associated with the manufacture of products.

Profit. See net income.

Profit margin. Net income expressed as a percentage of net sales.

Proprietorship. An unincorporated business with a single owner.

Quick assets. Current assets other than inventory and prepaid expenses.

Real account. An account with a balance after the closing process has been completed; it appears on the balance sheet.

Realization concept. An accounting concept which assumes that revenue is recognized when goods are delivered or services are performed, in an amount that is reasonably certain to be realized.

Recognize. The act of recording a revenue or expense item in a given accounting period.

Residual value. The amount for which a company expects to be able to sell a fixed asset at the end of its service life.

Retained earnings. The increase in the shareholders' equity as a result of profitable company operations.

Return. The amount earned on invested funds during a period.

Return on shareholders' investment. A ratio obtained by dividing the return by the average amount of shareholders' investment for the period.

Revenue. An increase in owners' equity resulting from operations.

Security. An instrument such as a stock or bond.

Service life. The period of time over which an asset is estimated to be of service to the company.

Shareholders. The owners of an incorporated business.

Solvency. The ability to meet long-term obligations.

Stated value. The amount that the directors decide is the value of no-par stock.

Statement of changes in financial position. A financial statement explaining the changes that have occurred in asset, liability, and owners' equity items in an accounting period.

Stock split. An exchange of the number of shares of stock outstanding for a larger number.

Straight line method. A depreciation method which charges off an equal fraction of the cost of a fixed asset over each year of its service life.

Taxable income. The amount of income subject to income tax, computed according to the rules of the Internal Revenue Service.

Transaction. A business event that is recorded in the accounting records.

Treasury stock. Previously issued stock that has been bought back by the company.

Write down. To reduce the cost of an item, especially inventory, to its market value.

Years'-digit method. An accelerated method of depreciation.

Index